SPERANZA

A Biography of Lady Wilde

SPERANZA, Lady Wilde

Painted by BERNARD MULRENIN, R.H.A.   *Engraved by WM. OLDHAM*

SPERANZA

A BIOGRAPHY OF LADY WILDE

by

HORACE WYNDHAM

LONDON ★ NEW YORK
T. V. BOARDMAN & COMPANY LIMITED
14 COCKSPUR STREET, LONDON, S.W.1

First Published 1951

This book is set in 12 *on* 14 *point Baskerville and printed and bound in Great Britain by the Hollen Street Press, Ltd., London, W.*1

CONTENTS

v

ILLUSTRATIONS

ACKNOWLEDGMENTS

In the "literary salons" of Bloomsbury and Chelsea the contention is commonly advanced that to quote a short passage from one existing book is plagiarism, but to quote a few long passages from half a dozen is research. This, however, is only reasonable, for, as anybody who has attempted biographical work is aware, it is often necessary to milk a hundred cows to extract even a small quantity of cream, that is, of cream that will bear the test of analysis.

To unravel, from the maze of fantasy and invention surrounding it, the career of Speranza, Lady Wilde, is not a simple task. Her story has never been written in full. Where she is concerned, there is nothing beyond scattered references in mid-Victorian memoirs and stray newspaper paragraphs. But few of these are entirely reliable, for they seldom agree as to names, dates, and places. Speranza's father, for example, is said in several of them to have been a Wexford clergyman, Archdeacon Elgee. He, however, was her grandfather; and it was his son, a Wexford solicitor, who was her father. Then, in respect of her literary output, a good deal for which she was not responsible is often attributed to her, just as a good deal for which she really was responsible is omitted.

For permission to include a number of hitherto unpublished letters written by Sir William Hamilton to Lady Wilde, I am indebted to Sir Sidney Orme Rowan-Hamilton; to Messrs Cassell for passages from *The Woman's World*, and *More Memories*, by Margot Asquith; to Messrs Jonathan Cape for a passage from *The Adventures of a Novelist*, by Gertrude Atherton; to Messrs Constable for a passage from *Forty Years in my Bookshop*, by Walter Spencer (edited by Thomas Moult); to Messrs Duckworth for a passage from *Oscar Wilde, a Summing-up*, by Lord Alfred Douglas; to the Harvard University Press for a passage from *Letters to the New Island*, by W. B. Yeats; to Messrs Heinemann for a passage from *Both Sides of the Curtain*, by Elizabeth Robins; to Vyvyan Holland for a passage from *Lord Arthur Savile's Crime*, by Oscar Wilde; to Henry Maxwell for a passage from *Time Gathered*, by W. B. Maxwell; to Messrs Hutchinson for a passage from *Celebrities and I*, by Henriette Corkran; to Messrs John Lane for a passage from *Fifty Years of Spoof*, by Arthur Roberts, and from *Some Victorian Women*, by Harry Furniss; to Messrs Werner Laurie for a passage from *Oscar Wilde*, by Robert Harborough Sherard, and from *Four Years*, and *The Trembling of a Veil*, by W. B. Yeats; to Messrs Methuen for a passage from *Jimmy Glover, his Book*, by James Glover; to Messrs John Murray for a passage from *Work and Days*, by Michael Field; and to Mrs Harry Furniss for the sketches of Sir William and Lady Wilde.

The other authorities consulted are, so far as they can be traced, given in footnotes on the pages to which they refer.

H. W.

"STRONG nations fight; oppressed nations sing; and thus, not with armies and fleets, but with the passionate storm of lyric words, have the Irish people kept up for centuries their ceaseless war against alien rule. For words have a mystic power over men; and, with the word Liberty on their lips, and the ideal of Nationhood in their hearts, the Irish have been preserved by their poets and orators from degenerating into the coarse vulgarisms of music and song so popular amongst a people who have no aspirations, no ideal beyond the greed of gain and the plenitude of all the sensuous enjoyments of life."

Notes on Men, Women, and Books.

—LADY WILDE.

CHAPTER I

RING UP THE CURTAIN

I

THAT once flourishing London institution, the literary *salon*, has long since disappeared, having, it would seem, been ousted by night clubs and bottle-parties, and crooners replacing conversation. Yet, fifty and sixty years ago quite a number of such "circles"— with young bloods and old bloods, authors and artists, musicians and mummers, and playwrights and poets revolving round them and endeavouring to set the Thames on fire—were in full swing, some in Belgravia, some in Bloomsbury, and others functioning in the hinterlands of Chelsea and St. John's Wood.

Among the would-be Madame Récamiers conducting these assemblies, there was one figure that, still remembered by the older generation, stood out prominently among them. This was that of the woman who, known in the non-literary world as Lady Wilde, elected, on joining the literary one, to adopt for her books and poems and magazine contributions the *nom de guerre* Speranza.

2

There are many biographical slips and unwarrantable embroideries woven round the origin of the young Irish girl who began life as Jane Francesca Elgee and ended it as Lady Wilde. Among the commonest of such slips is the often repeated one that she was born the daughter of a distinguished Irish clergyman, Archdeacon Elgee, of County Wexford. Since, however, the Archdeacon died three years before she was born, this assertion would appear unfounded. It was unfounded, for she was his grand-daughter; and it was his eldest son, Charles, a Wexford attorney, who married a Miss Kingsbury, who was her father. She had no sisters, and her only brother, anxious to improve his position, went to America. There he took out papers of naturalization, and, joining the New York Bar, eventually became a judge.

Jane Francesca Elgee, the future Lady Wilde, always told enquirers that she was born in 1826. The contention, however, was incorrect, and was due to the fact that she had adopted the feminine prerogative of lopping a couple of years off her real age, an example followed in after years by her son Oscar.

Beyond her father's family, Charles Elgee's daughter had a number of relatives who had distinguished themselves in various directions. Thus, one of her uncles was Sir Charles Ormsby, a Member of Parliament; and a cousin, Sir Robert McClure, accompanied the expedition that was sent to look for (but which failed to find) Sir John Franklin and his comrades who had disappeared somewhere in the Arctic Circle. She was also a grand-niece of a well-known man of letters, Charles Maturin,* a friend of Scott and Byron, and alluded to by name in *Endymion*.

This Charles Maturin, born in Dublin in 1782 and educated at Trinity College, was a grandson of Dean Swift's successor as Dean of St. Patrick's Cathedral. Many-sided, he became in turn clergyman, school-

---

* "Melmoth" was the name of a character in one of Maturin's novels. Preceded by "Sebastian", this name was, after his downfall, assumed by Oscar Wilde; and he was commonly known by it during his last years, first, in Berneval and afterwards in Paris.

master, novelist, and playwright. As a dramatist, he had a tragedy produced by Edmund Kean at Drury Lane, after Kemble had declined it; and two other tragedies from his pen, with Macready appearing in one of them, were staged at Covent Garden. Of his novels the best known was his *Melmoth the Wanderer*, which has been described (not unfairly) as "a compound of *Faust* and *The Wandering Jew*". Still, whatever it owed (which was a good deal) to Goethe and Eugène Sue, the novel enjoyed a considerable sale, especially in France, where it attracted the attention of Balzac, who wrote a continuation of it under a different title.

We all have our little weaknesses, especially when it offers a prospect of adding to our importance. Jane Francesca Elgee had hers, full measure of them; and, to the confusion of the genealogists, was in after years given to claim an Italian origin. In support of this contention she would assert that the Elgee family was formerly Algiati and was that born by her great grandfather. At times she would improve on this and even claim descent from Dante Alighieri. But this was a characteristic delusion. Her forebears on either side were one and all Hibernian, with not a single Florentine among any of them.

As a mere child Charles Elgee's daughter was remarkably precocious. Thus, at an age when other little girls of her years were playing with dolls and looking at picture books this one was reading Latin and Greek "for pleasure". Taught by a succession of governesses and tutors, she also managed to acquire a sound knowledge of French, German, and Italian; and (so it was claimed for her) "could discuss in an intelligent fashion politics and literature with her father's friends".

Instead of being snubbed, and, as was the custom in those days, told that "little girls should be seen and not heard", this one was allowed to ask questions and offer her own views on any subject engaging her elders. She read voraciously, and early amassed a considerable stock of general knowledge, especially where history and languages were concerned. "I want to know," she would say to her governesses. "Why don't you tell me?"

There were times when she puzzled those who were responsible for her education and found her demands for enlightenment beyond them. On one occasion, failing to get some information on a subject in which she was interested, she delivered an ultimatum to her governess : "If you won't educate me, I'll educate myself." To a certain extent she succeeded; but for the most part her efforts resulted in little beyond acquiring a stock of miscellaneous knowledge that had no practical value. Yet, at the age of fifteen she was not far removed from developing into a "bluestocking". In after years there was something of a parallel between her precociousness and that of Sir William Rowan-Hamilton, the distinguished mathematician and philosopher with whom she was to become closely acquainted.

"What are you going to do with yourself when you grow up?" enquired one of her father's friends as he saw her immersed in some solid looking volumes.

"I shall write poetry," was the answer.

"Anything else?"

"Yes, travel books and history about Ireland."

3

As she left girlhood behind her, Jane Francesca Elgee grew up into a tall, striking-looking young

SPERANZA of " The Nation "

CHARLES GAVAN DUFFY
Editor of " The Nation "

woman, with raven hair, dark flashing eyes and a well-formed figure. Her main interests were concentrated on politics and history, more especially where they concerned her own country. She read everything on the subject she could find in her father's library, or in the books and pamphlets she could borrow from his friends. Her sympathies were always with the underdog. "Enthusiasm in the heart of a woman is," she wrote, "like the fire in the Temple of Vesta, once kindled, ever burning." Indeed, her enthusiasm was such that she adopted *Fidanza, Constanza, Speranza* for her motto, and made every effort to live up to it.

A descriptive note on this subject was that of Martin MacDermott:

"A young lady of fashion, the daughter of a dignitary of the Irish Church*—Miss Jane Francesca Elgee—could scarcely have been taught to regard with sympathy the native poor people whom she saw suffering around her, or the men who had embraced their cause. But, in the end, no voice that was raised in the cause of the poor and the oppressed; none that denounced political wrong-doing in Ireland was more eagerly listened to than that of the graceful and accomplished woman known in literature as Speranza, and in society as Lady Wilde."

It is difficult to discover why MacDermott, Gavan Duffy and Sullivan, and—for that matter—many others who ought to have known better—should say that Miss Elgee's father was a clergyman. She herself always said he was not. Her opinion was correct, for, as has been noted, Charles Elgee was an attorney with a practice in Wexford.

---

* An often repeated error.

4

She did not know it, but a young Dublin journalist with whom Miss Elgee, then a girl of sixteen, was soon to be associated—and with results that were to write an eventful chapter in both their lives—was already at work behind the scenes. This was Charles Gavan Duffy, an ardent Nationalist by conviction, who, with a band of others sharing his views, had formed a project to launch a paper which should voice their country's needs. The necessary capital (then much more modest than would now be required) was secured, a title selected, and Gavan Duffy appointed editor, with a well-chosen staff of contributors.* As he believed in young blood and plenty of it, all his assistants were under thirty, and he himself was twenty-six.

The birth of the new venture, to be known as THE NATION was heralded in a prospectus with a characteristic flourish of trumpets :

"The proprietors have been told that there is no room in Ireland for yet another Liberal organ. But they think differently . . . The necessities of the country seem to demand a journal able to aid and organize the new movement going on amongst us . . . Such a journal should be free from the quarrels, the interests, the wrongs, and even the gratitude of the past. It should be free to apply its strength where it seems best; free to praise; free to censure, unshackled by sect or party.

"Holding these views, the proprietors of THE

---

* "The group of young men, who, under the editorship of Gavan Duffy, conducted the 'Nation', were," wrote W. E. H. Lecky, "men who in any country and in any time would have made their mark."

NATION cannot think that a journal prepared to undertake this work will be deemed superfluous; and, as they labour, not for themselves, but for their country, they are prepared, if they do not find a way open, to try if they cannot make one. "

In short, the editorial policy was "to create and foster public opinion in Ireland and make it racy of the soil".

An ambitious programme; and, among the claims put forward to attract readers was one declaring that "the services of the most eminent political writers in the country have been secured". This was no idle boast, for the staff included William Carleton, Thomas Davis, John Blake Dillon, Denis MacCarthy, Clarence Mangan, Thomas MacNeven, John O'Hagan, Richard Dalton Williams, and others of similar calibre. Altogether, a strong team.

With Gavan Duffy to direct affairs at the helm, and an accomplished band of contributors working for him, THE NATION soon got over its birth pangs and settled down into a financial success. "The reception of the journal among the cultivated classes," wrote the editor, "is intelligible; but it was a marvel then, and it is still a marvel, how quickly it seized upon the classes to whom reading was not a necessity."

5

THE NATION, which made its bow to the public on October 15, 1842, was conducted on lines that were then distinctly novel in journalism. Thus, contributors were remunerated handsomely; advertisements of quack nostrums and financial schemes were not admitted to its columns; and, to ensure unbiased criticism, tickets for admission to the theatre were charged to the office. None the less, the policy

answered, and the circulation soon reached a satisfactory figure.

It was in connection with its attitude towards
alleged cure-alls that THE NATION was once involved in
legal proceedings. During an unguarded moment a
Dublin apothecary managed to get inserted an
advertisement of some pills "guaranteed to cure
sufferers from bowel complaints". When he saw it,
the editor printed a notice, "expressing regret for
admitting a quack advertisement to his columns".
Thereupon, the indignant pill-maker brought an
action for "malicious libel". Although expert evidence was called to prove that the pills "had nothing in
them but soap and bread crumbs" the jury found for
the plaintiff and awarded him forty shillings damages.
Duffy was not upset by the verdict. "Perhaps," he
wrote, "the gentlemen of England, who live at home
at ease, may understand, from transactions like these,
why English law in Ireland, administered by ascendancy judges, has not won all the veneration to which
they esteem it entitled."

"THE NATION," remarked its editor, "was not a
journal designed to chronicle the small beer of current
politics, but to inform public opinion, and this was a
task never neglected . . . Every line of the contents
passed under my eye. No one was assailed for any
offence except some public delinquency injurious to
Ireland, and no one assailed was ever refused a
hearing. The aim of THE NATION* was speedily

---

* "THE NATION newspaper, which was conducted and written for by some
rising young men of high culture and remarkable talent, had long been written
in a style of romantic and sentimental nationalism which could hardly give
much satisfaction from the somewhat cunning and ticklish agitation which
O'Connell had set going. THE NATION and the clever youths who wrote for
it were all for nationalism of the Hellenic or French type, and were disposed
to laugh at constitutional agitation and to chafe against the influence of the
priests." *A History of our own Times*: Justin McCarthy.

understood by the best men in Ireland; they recognized almost instinctively that here was a journal that was not a commercial speculation, but the voice of men to whom the elevation of Ireland was a creed and a passion."

As was perhaps to be expected, a certain amount of adverse criticism met the fledgling. John O'Connell, for example, complained that "Father Prout" was unduly belauded, while Samuel Lover was ignored; and a rival editor asserted that the "dangerous songs" in its columns were contributed by Tom Moore. Then the *Quarterly Review* ("savage and tartarly") pronounced the literary contents to be "perilous and mischievous because they were the actual convictions of the writers"; and a third critic solemnly declared, "We regard, and we are not singular in this view, THE NATION as the most formidable phenomenon of these strange and menacing times."

On the other hand, W. E. H. Lecky, although the staunchest of staunch Unionists, could give the new-comer his warm approval. "Seldom," he wrote, "has any journal of the kind exhibited a more splendid combination of eloquence, of poetry, and of reasoning."

During the course of a political meeting held in Limerick somebody, disagreeing with a remark he had made, threw a stone at Smith O'Brien. When she heard of it Miss Elgee wrote an indignant letter to Gavan Duffy :

"What can be done with such idiots and savages? The noble Smith O'Brien, who has sacrificed all for the people, and who could gain nothing in return, for no position however exalted could add to his dignity, whose life has been a sacrifice to his country,

a self-immolation.   And this is the man who has to
be guarded by the English from Irish murderers!
I cannot endure to think of it.   We are disgraced
for ever before Europe, and justly so.   Adieu!"

It was in the columns of his journal that Gavan
Duffy added to the cares of editorship by contributing
a number of his own poems.   "None of the Young
Irelanders," says T. W. Rolleston, "wrote in rhyme
and metre with more sinewy force than Duffy.   His
lines smote home like the arc of an Irish gallowglass;
and though his mind, as his whole career shows, was
eminently that of a statesman, he clearly thought and
felt as a reckless fighter when he faced the enemies of
his cause with the keen blade of verse in his hand."

CHAPTER 2

POLITICS AND POETRY

I

THE year 1848 was everywhere a troubled one; a witches' cauldron threatening to boil over; fire and sword sweeping across half Europe; and the chancelleries disturbing the old dynasties and evolving fresh ones in all directions. The general spirit of unrest soon spread to Ireland. This, however, was not remarkable, for the conditions obtaining there among the peasantry were almost beyond belief. "It is difficult," says an historian, "to describe them without seeming to employ the language of exaggeration. All external symbols of nationality were nearly as effectually banished from Dublin as they were banished from Warsaw under the Cossack, or from Venice under the Austrian."

In Ireland the whole country from end to end quivered under a combination of blight and landlordism of the worst description. No help of any sort was forthcoming from England. On the contrary, Parliament, backed up by Lord John Russell and Sir Robert Peel and the rest of the Cabinet, held it an article of faith that the agrarian outrages for which the misery and despair of the people were responsible could only be suppressed by rushing through a Coercion Bill which would have been unduly severe if directed by the Czar against a band of Nihilists.

A factor largely responsible for the unhappy situation of the country at this period was the systematic neglect of education. For the peasant class it was the hedge school, or nothing, generally nothing. "The instruction of the children of the poor," wrote William Carleton, "was a matter in which no one took any interest. The Irishman was not only not educated, but was actually punished for attempting to acquire knowledge in the first place; and, in the second, punished for the ignorance created by its absence. In other words, the penal laws rendered education criminal, and then caused the unhappy people to suffer for the crimes which proper knowledge would have prevented them from committing. Nor is it any wonder if poverty and ignorance combined should give the country a character for turbulence and outrage."

Writing on this subject years afterwards, Miss Elgee had something to say :

"The fervent nationality evoked by Moore's music and song at the opening of the century, and formulated afterwards into an immense political force by O'Connell, rose to a fever of enthusiasm in 1848, when a madness of lyrical passion seemed to sweep over the heart of the nation. . . . Even Trinity College struck the Irish harp to Hymns of Freedom, and the most popular poem of that era, 'Who Fears to Speak of Ninety-Eight?' was written by a young Collegian, afterwards a distinguished Fellow of the University."

The "lyrical passion" to which she alluded found its chief exponents in William Carleton, Samuel Ferguson, Clarence Mangan, Aubrey de Vere, and John Waller.

2

In after years—when she was Lady Wilde—Jane Francesca Elgee told an interviewer that it was not until she was seventeen that she felt any inclination towards authorship. By chance she then picked up on a Dublin bookstall a copy of a pamphlet written by Richard Dalton Williams in the interests of the Nationalist movement. What she read there set a spark to her own sense of patriotism and fired her with a sympathy for the cause advanced by Williams. "Then it was," she said, "that I discovered I could write poetry." In fact, she was so convinced that she possessed the gift that she strung together some verses, signed "John Fenshaw Ellis", and dropped them into the letter-box of THE NATION.

According to D. J. O'Donoghue, the Librarian of University College, Dublin, this particular effort, with the signature "John Fenshaw Ellis" attached to it, appeared in the issue for October 26, 1844, and was entitled "The Chosen Leader". This, however, is questionable, for not only did she herself repudiate its authorship, but a number of other items commonly attributed to her were really written by somebody else who adopted the same *nom de guerre*. Among such may be mentioned a long dramatic poem dealing with the career of Ugo Bassi, the Italian patriot and revolutionary. Miss Elgee's reason for adopting the signature "John Fenshaw Ellis" was that, on the deaths of her parents, she went to live with an uncle who, being a staunch Unionist, regarded THE NATION as a "seditious rag" and would not permit a copy in his house.

It was somewhere about the year 1847 that Miss

Elgee's first poem was published in THE NATION.
Overjoyed at thus seeing herself in print, other efforts
soon followed this initial one. Signed as before,
"John Fenshaw Ellis", they were all marked by a
passionate fervour, and all found ready acceptance.

Among samples of her Muse, at this period, the
following are typical :

TO IRELAND

My country, wounded to the heart,
Could I but flash along thy soul
   Electric power to rive apart
The thunder-clouds that round thee roll,
And, by my burning words, uplift
Thy life from out Death's icy drift,
Till the full splendours of our age
Shone round thee for thy heritage—
As Miriam's, by the Red Sea strand
Clashing proud cymbals, so my hand
    Would strike thy harp,
    Loved Ireland!
  In glorious chants for freedom won,
While over Pharaoh's gilded cars
   The fierce, death-bearing waves rolled on;
I can but look in God's great face,
And pray Him for our fated race,
To come in Sinai thunders down,
And, with His mystic radiance, crown
Some Prophet-Leader, with command
To break the strength of Egypt's band,
    And set thee free,
    Loved Ireland!

THE YEAR OF REVOLUTIONS

I

Lift up your pale faces, ye children of sorrow,
The night passes on to a glorious to-morrow!
Hark! hear you not sounding glad Liberty's pæan,
From the Alps to the Isles of the tideless Ægean?
And the rhythmical march of the gathering nations,
And the crashing of thrones 'neath their fierce
  exultations,
And the cry of Humanity cleaving the ether,
With hymns of the conquering rising together—
God, Liberty, Truth! How they burn heart and
  brain—
These words shall they burn—shall they waken in
  vain?

II

No! soul answers soul, steel flashes on steel,
And land wakens land with a grand thunder-peal.
Shall we, oh! my Brothers, but weep, pray, and
  groan,
When France reads her rights by the flames of a
  Throne?
Shall we fear and falter to join the grand chorus,
When Europe has trod the dark pathway before us?
Oh, courage! and we, too, will trample them down,
The minions of power, the serfs of a crown.
Oh, courage! but courage, if once to the winds
Ye fling Freedom's banner, no tyranny binds.

III

At the voice of the people the weak symbols fall,
And Humanity marches o'er purple and pall,
O'er sceptre and crown, with a glorious disdain,

For the symbol must fall and Humanity reign.
Onward! then onward! ye brave to the vanguard,
Gather in glory round Liberty's standard!
Like France, lordly France, we shall sweep from
  their station
All, all who oppose the stern will of a nation;
Like Prussia's brave children will stoop to no lord,
But demand our just rights at the point of the sword.

An effort in what Gavan Duffy called "the high
heroic mood" was the following:

Oh! that I stood upon some lofty tower,
Before the gathered people face to face,
That, like God's thunder, might my words of power
Roll down the cry of freedom to its base!
Oh! that my voice, a storm above all storms
Could cleave earth, air and ocean, rend the sky
With fierce shout, "To Arms! To Arms!"
For Truth, Fame, Freedom, Vengeance, Victory!

This was certainly inflammatory, if nothing else.
Once more the editor's description was "a high heroic
effort". Encouraged by such appreciation, Speranza was delivered of further samples, all of which
Gavan Duffy was glad to print.

One of the last poems* she contributed to THE
NATION was an address to her countrymen, calling on
them to be "Up and Doing!"

3

Speranza, as the new recruit elected (alter-
natively with "John Fenshaw Ellis") to call herself,

---

* It is recorded that Thomas Davis "opposed the introduction of verse when
this journal was started". The opposition, however, did not survive beyond
the first two numbers; and to those that followed Davis himself contributed
several poems.

was one of a quartet of sister poets appearing in THE NATION, the other three members being Ellen Mary Downing, Eva Mary Kelly, and Olivia Knight. Discussing their work, A. M. Sullivan, the author of *New Ireland*, says of it :

"Speranza—then Miss Elgee, now Lady Wilde— was incomparably the most brilliant of the galaxy. . . . Young, beautiful, highly educated, endowed with the rarest gifts of intellect, her personal attractions, her cultivated mind, her originality and force of character made her the central figure in Dublin society thirty years ago."

For all that he was something of a poet himself, and a sound critic, Stopford Brooke could write of Speranza's contributions :

"The passionate rhetoric of her verse, which reflected her own fearless and generous character, helped in no small degree to make THE NATION a political force; but, as in the case of many other writers of both prose and verse, she won her true literary success in the former medium."

Another critic, Martin MacDermott, went further— a lot further : "Her poems are largely characterized by a certain epic or Scriptural largeness of utterance— a sweeping and overmastering melody and a strain of majestic thought. Womanlike, she has a heart 'open as the day to melting charity'. The sights and scenes of the famine year appear to have gone through her with the sharpness of a sword."*

Thus encouraged, half the would-be bards and bardlets within a hundred miles of Dublin wanted to appear in the columns of THE NATION. As a result,

---

* "The passionate rhetoric of her verses, which reflected her own fearless and generous character, helped in no small degree to make the *Nation* a political force." *Irish Literature*, Justin McCarthy.

the editorial desk was cluttered up with their offerings. "I can still," said Gavan Duffy, "recall the mixture of delight and alarm with which I read the contributions from new correspondents, so striking and effective, so far above the range of Poets' Corner verses, that I was tormented by a suspicion that they must be plagiarisms or adaptations of poems which had escaped my reading."

But this was not the only trouble confronting the editor, for the surfeit was objected to by the printers, who wanted to charge for setting up poetry as if it were prose, that is, as if each line filled the width of a column. The editor announced that, sooner than yield to such a demand, he would dismiss the lot of them and stop the paper. This firm attitude soon brought the composing-room staff to their senses.

When she fleshed her maiden pen in the columns of THE NATION, the young contributor was living in Leeson Street, Dublin, with an uncle. It was from No. 34 there that the signature, "John Fenshaw Ellis", which she attached to her early efforts, conveyed little to their recipient. Curious to make the personal acquaintance of the writer, Duffy inserted a request to this effect in a column headed, "Notices to Correspondents". This had the desired effect, and a meeting was arranged. An interesting account of it is recorded by Gavan Duffy in his *Four Years of Irish History*.

"Another poetess came in a widely different guise. Her virile and sonorous songs broke on the public's ear like the plash in later times of a great wave of thought in one of Swinburne's metres. . . . I was greatly struck by the first contribution, and requested Mr. John Fenshaw Ellis to call at THE NATION Office. Mr. Ellis pleaded that there were difficulties which

rendered this course impracticable, and invited me to
visit him in Leeson Street. I did so immediately, not
without a secret suspicion of the transformation I was
about to witness. A smiling parlourmaid, when I
enquired for Mr. Ellis, showed me into a drawing-room,
where I found only Mr. George Smith, publisher to
the University. 'What!' I cried, 'my loyal friend, are
you the new volcano of sedition?' Mr. Smith only
answered by vanishing into a back drawing-room and
returning with a tall girl on his arm, whose stately
carriage and figure, flashing brown eyes, and features
cast in an heroic mould, seemed fit for the genius of
poetry or the spirit of revolution. He presented me
to Miss Jane Francesca Elgee, in lieu of Mr. John
Fenshaw Ellis. Miss Elgee was the daughter of an
archdeacon of the Establishment [sic], and had
probably heard nothing of Irish nationality among
her ordinary associates, but, as the strong and generous
are apt to do, had worked out convictions for herself . . . Her little scented notes, sealed with wax of
a delicate hue and dainty device, represented a
substantial force in Irish politics, the vehement will of
a woman of genius."*

Charles Read, in his *Cabinet of Irish Literature*, said
much the same thing :

"In addition to her poetical contributions, there
also came from her hand some of the most daring
effective and vehement press articles of THE NATION."

By the way, as indicative of the flood of inac-
curacies prevalent about the career of Speranza,
A. M. Sullivan, who ought to have known better, says
that when Gavan Duffy called at 34, Leeson Street,
to make her acquaintance, he was "introduced to her

---

* A somewhat different opinion was expressed by *The Times*: "She became
the most ardent and hot-headed of Nationalists."

by her husband, Dr. Wilde, whom she married in
1845". There are two quite adequate reasons for not
accepting this off-hand. One is that Dr. Wilde was
then living in Westland Row, with his sister Emily;
and the other is that he did not marry until 1851.
Apart from this, the Dublin Directory gives another
name as the occupant of No. 34 Leeson Street. But
Gavan Duffy himself is not always accurate, for he is
in error in saying that his new contributor was "the
stately daughter of an archdeacon of the Established
Church". Since, however, it was not until three
years after the death of this cleric that Miss Elgee was
born, her birth would suggest delayed action on the
part of Mrs. Archdeacon to a degree hitherto unknown
in obstetrical history.

Having a considerable number of books for review,
Duffy sent the newcomer to the fold a copy of Philip
James Bailey's *Festus*, and enquired her opinion of
this curious mixture of philosophy and theology.
"It is," was her verdict, "superb, lofty as heaven and
deep as inspiration. I read two scenes to-day that
made me grow pale with wonder". The editorial
reaction to this criticism was, "it needs a liberal
allowance for the perfervor commonly incident to a
woman of genius."

It was from Leeson Street that Miss Elgee wrote to
Duffy about another book he had sent her :

34 Leeson Street, Monday

My Dear Sir :—I return, with many thanks, the
volume of Cromwell, which has been travelling
about with me for the last four months, and shall
feel much obliged for the two others when you are
quite at leisure, though not even Carlyle can make
this soulless iconoclast interesting. It is the only

work of Carlyle's I have met with in which my heart does not go along with his words.

I cannot forbear telling you, now the pen is in my hand, how deeply impressed I felt by your opening lecture to your club. It was the sublimest teaching and the style so simple from its very sublimity—it seemed as if Truth passed directly from your heart to ours without the aid of any medium—at least I felt that everywhere the *thoughts* struck you, nowhere the *words*, and this in my opinion is the perfection of composition. It is soul speaking to soul. I never felt the dignity of your cause so much as then—to promote it in any way seemed an object that would ennoble a life. Truly, one cannot despair when God sends us such teachers. But you will wish me away again for another four months if I write you such long notes. So I shall conclude with kind compliments to Mrs. Duffy, and remain yours very sincerely, FRANCESCA ELGEE.

I only *read* your lecture—some time or other I would like to *hear* you.

Every now and again, Duffy, like other editors, had a little trouble with his team of contributors. Some of them wanted to go their own way, which was not always his. Speranza, he once said, "had not lost sympathy with the National cause, but she had not unnaturally lost hope, and was indignant with the people at large. 'I do not blame the leaders in the least,' she wrote to me. 'In Sicily or Belgium they would have been successful.' To my policy and projects she gave a general, but tepid, assent and sympathy; but the eagerness and impatience of a woman of genius could ill reconcile themselves to the slow road we were bound to travel."

There was, however, one of Duffy's projects which met with her enthusiastic approval. This was to form a "Small Proprietors' Society", in accordance with a scheme he had prepared. "I have read the pamphlet with great interest," she wrote. "If the object can be accomplished, it will make Ireland a 'Garden of the Lord'. Nothing so admirable has ever yet been suggested. But the Small Estates should be guarded against subletting, or we shall have renewed cycles of pauperism only."

CHAPTER 3

SOUNDING THE TOCSIN

I

GAVAN DUFFY once described the general tone of Speranza's writings as "vehement". It was more than this, for the keynote of practically all her contributions—whether of prose or verse—to THE NATION was a virile and passionate rhetoric, often tinged with something perilously near rhodomontade. A good deal of it, too, was not far removed from fustian. But it none the less aroused an interest beyond Dublin. "Specimens of the prose and poetry appearing in THE NATION were," says Duffy (but without any authority for the assertion), "read in the House of Commons, as significant evidence of a new spirit more dangerous than the traditional and manageable agitations of the past."

Officialdom shared this view and was quick to act. Armed with a search warrant, the police paid a surprise visit to the editorial sanctum and carried off a number of manuscripts, which might be held by the Castle authorities to be suspect. "One of them," says Gavan Duffy, "excited extraordinary interest when it became known to be the writing of a woman. It was lofty and passionate as one of Napoleon's bulletins after a great victory. This was a leading article, *Jacta Alea Est*, signed Speranza."

"It was," wrote A. M. Sullivan, "without example as a revolutionary appeal. Exquisitely beautiful as a piece of writing, it glowed with fiery invective. It

was, in fact, a prose poem, a wild war song, in which
Ireland was called upon that day in the face of earth
and heaven to invoke the *ultima ratio* of oppressed
nations."

It should, however, be pointed out that more
critical judges did not share in this panegyric. George
Woodcock, for example, in his *The Paradox of Oscar
Wilde*, describes the *Jacta Alea Est* outburst as "somewhat verbose and florid . . . little more than rather
flatulent ranting". Present-day sober judgment sup-
ports this opinion.

More than twenty years later an enterprising
editor, wishing to reprint the article, as it had again
become topical, sent the author a proof for revision.
It was returned to him unread, with the comment,
"I cannot now tread the ashes of that once glowing
past".

Miss Elgee's contribution, when set up in type, ran
to about 6,000 words, and the issue of THE NATION in
which it appeared (July 29, 1848) was immediately
suppressed by the Castle authorities, and anybody
found selling a copy ran the risk of being prosecuted.
Still, people were prepared to take the risk; and a
transcript of the article in its entirety from a copy of
the issue containing it in the National Library of
Ireland in Dublin is given in the Appendix.

The Castle authorities, fearful of further inflammatory material from the same pen, shivered in their
shoes; and an order was signed by Lord Clarendon,
the Viceroy, to suppress THE NATION and bring its
editor to trial on a charge of treason-felony.

When Speranza's contribution was set up Gavan
Duffy was not in the office, as he had, under the
suspension of the Habeas Corpus Act, already been
arrested and was languishing in the Dublin bridewell.

The paper, however, was being carried on for him by other hands. His sister-in-law, Margaret Callan, temporarily took over the editorship; "and", she says, "Miss Elgee (Speranza) promised a leading article suitable to the occasion, and provided one which might be issued from the headquarters of the national army. It can no more be judged by detached fragments than a stately edifice by the coping-stone". The article (*Jacta Alea Est*) was, says Duffy, "smuggled out of prison". A second article, "The Tocsin of Ireland", being "another appeal to the people", was, without the knowledge of the authorities, also "smuggled" and printed in the same number. There would thus appear to have been a good deal of slackness among the prison staff.

While he was under lock and key, the Dublin correspondent of the *Daily News* reported that Gavan Duffy "was prepared to plead guilty to whatever indictment the Crown may prefer against him, throwing himself on the mercy of the Executive to dispose of him as may seem fitting in the case of one who does not even question its authority, much less offer any opposition to its paramount operation".

As there was not a word of truth in this, its subject, when he heard of it, was furious. "I would," he declared, "rather have forfeited my life than endure this charge in silence." With the help of one of his counsel he managed to send a letter to the *Freeman's Journal*, "denouncing the falsehood with not unjust indignation". The denial upset Lord Clarendon, "who wrote with his own hand to the Prison Board, complaining that I had been permitted to send out such a letter".

2

The trial of Gavan Duffy was held before Baron
Richards and Mr. Justice Perrin, with the prosecution
conducted by the Attorney-General, and the defence
by Sir Colman O'Loghlen and Isaac Butt, Q.C.*
As the grand jury returned true bills, the arraignment
began; and, since the Crown was determined to leave
no loophole, there were six separate counts in the
indictment. They were all serious, but by far the
most serious one among them was that of treason-
felony, in respect of "contriving and compassing to
depose Our Sovereign Lady the Queen and to levy
war against her Majesty, her Crown and Dignity".
A hanging matter had a verdict of guilty been
delivered.

The panel from which had to be chosen the jurors
in the case of "The Queen against Duffy" was perhaps
an oddly selected one. Thus, among those summoned
on it were the Lord-Lieutenant's hairdresser, a watch
and clock winder, a shoemaker, the Castle grocer and
tea merchant, two choristers from St. Patrick's
Cathedral, and the French consul in Dublin. A
number of these were successfully challenged on
various grounds, and much time was occupied in
securing twelve others to whom no objection was
advanced.

When the Attorney-General, rising in his wrath and
pressing for a conviction, read a passage from the

---

* Isaac Butt was a member of both the English and the Irish Bar; and is
credited with having been the first to adopt the expression Home Rule in a
political speech.   In 1871 he wrote, under a pseudonym, a pamphlet, *What
does she do with It?* as "No. 1 Tract for the Times by Solomon Temple".   This
took the form of a violent criticism of the Royal grants; and was bitterly
resented by the Queen.   Had his authorship of the pamphlet been known to
her Majesty, his appointment as Q.C. would have been imperilled, if not
cancelled.

famous *Jacta Alea Est* article, Miss Elgee, sitting
unsuspected in the public gallery, sprang up, and, to
the astonishment of all, interrupted him.

"Pray, who are you, madam?" demanded the Chief
Justice when he had got over his surprise.

"I am the criminal who, as the author of the article
that had just been read, should be in the dock," was
the calm answer. "Any blame in respect of it belongs
to me."

"You must be good enough to keep quiet," returned
his lordship. "That is," he added warningly, "unless
you wish to be committed to prison for contempt of
court."

Isaac Butt, who was counsel for Gavan Duffy, saw
his chance and took it eagerly.

"May it please your Lordship," he said, producing
an envelope, "I hold in my hand a letter from the
authoress of these articles, assuring me that Mr. Duffy
never saw any of them before they were published; and
that he was in prison at the time. I would not care to
give pain to the highly respectable connections of this
lady and to herself by placing her in the witness-box,
but I ask the Attorney-General, as a man of honour—
and a man of honour I believe him to be—he knows
the lady as well as I do—to contradict my statement
if it is not true."

The statement was accepted without demur. Nor
was there any further occasion to interrupt, for the
indictment had been so carelessly drawn that Gavan
Duffy was hauled before five separate Commissions of
Oyer and Terminer without a verdict being secured.
Feeling that one never would be secured, the Government then made the best of a bad job and abandoned
the prosecution. As a matter of fact, nobody had
really expected anything else.

"Glorious are the uncertainties of the law, and nowhere more gloriously uncertain than in this island of saints," was the comment of the Dublin correspondent of *The Times*. "While all Ireland will rejoice," added a second chronicler, "Great Britain will not be sorry to hear no more of Gavan Duffy."

As it happened, however, a good deal more was heard of Gavan Duffy. Profiting by his narrow escape from the clutches of the law, he changed his tactics; and, while still battling for reforms, he adopted less violent methods for securing them.

To be quite fair to him, it should be recorded of Gavan Duffy that if he did alter his political views it was for the best motives; and, a staunch patriot, he always put what he conceived to be the best interests of his country first. Thus, when after its temporary suppression, he revived THE NATION in 1849, he adopted constitutional methods of agitation; and, with the help of Frederick Lucas, he founded the Tenant League, the object of which was to assist small proprietors and protect them from the rapacity of the big landlords. Securing pledges of support, at the general election of 1852 he was returned as Member for New Ross. When, in 1856, on the death of Lucas, his plans were upset by office-seekers, anxious to feather their own nests and secure snug billets for themselves, he resigned his seat and went to Australia.*

Having by this time had enough of politics, he began to practise at the Bar in Melbourne. Before long, however, he was persuaded to enter the House of Assembly, where, says the *Catholic Encyclopædia*, "his

---

* When he was on the point of sailing, a public banquet was arranged in his honour. Among those attending was Carlyle, who wrote: "I have a real regard and even affection for Duffy, whose fine truthful intellect and ardent human character were always recognizable to me in the worst tumults of Irish confusions" : *Irish Booklover*.

great abilities made him a prominent figure. He filled in succession the position of Minister of Public Works and Minister of Public Lands, and for a brief period was Prime Minister . . . These honours and dignities he reached without ever denying either his country or his faith, or ever failing to defend them when assailed. He consistently championed the labourers and the farmers against the capitalists and squatters, and when he left Victoria in 1880 the whole colony regarded him as one of the ablest and most useful of her public men." In 1877 he was made a K.C.M.G. for his political services and elected Speaker of the House of Assembly. A difference of opinion with the Premier led him to resign this office and in 1880 to return to Europe.

In 1882 Gavan Duffy, then living in the south of France, to which country he had retired for health reasons, published his *Bird's-eye View of Irish History*. This work, with its masterly distillation of the essence of the subject he had at heart, proved an outstanding and well deserved success. On his death, which occurred on February 9, 1903, he was buried in Glasnevin cemetery, Dublin, near the grave of Charles Stewart Parnell, "Ireland's Uncrowned King", his junior by thirty years.

3

The cessation from publication of THE NATION in 1848 did not necessarily mean an end to the literary ambitions of Duffy's star contributor. As a matter of fact it had the effect of spurring on Speranza to fresh efforts. In 1852 she brought out her first travel book, *The Glacier Land*, which was announced by the publisher as "From the French of A. Dumas, by Mrs. R. W.

Wilde". This was followed by other translations, as well as by a number of original contributions that met with prompt acceptance from the editors of the Dublin magazines to which they were offered.

It was, by the way, in the footsteps of Calliope, Euterpe, and Polyhymnia that Speranza found a remedy for the manifold wrongs of her native land. Hence, she was prepared, after a cursory glance at its contents, to approve the action of the Irish Commissioners of Education in giving their imprimatur to a collection of poems "intended expressly for young hearts who are to be the working heads of the advancing age". When, however, she examined the volume critically, she registered disapproval. "There is not," she declared, "one single verse which would strike into the young Irish heart; and for the names of even our leading Irish writers we may search in vain." This was true enough, for, although the editor could declare "on the love of home is founded that of country", the solitary example offered the Irish child was "The Stately Homes of England"; and while Tom Moore was represented by only one item in the section headed "Songs and Lyrics", there were several by such poetasters as Eliza Cook (with her "Lines to a Butter-cup"), Mrs. Hemans,* and Letitia Landon.

The path of authorship is not always smooth; and there was an occasion when this candidate for its prizes crossed swords with a publisher. Gavan Duffy has an odd account of the episode :

"Speranza once committed a task to me which led me in the end into an awkward position. The editor of Bohn's Library was publishing a volume of trans-

---

* In a sketch of Mrs. Hemans, the author of *Illustrious Irishwomen* says: "There is no record of any other Irish woman—save the Speranza of our own day—having so successfully wooed the Muse."

lations from Schiller, and she wished me to offer a translation of 'Love and Cabal', which she had written, to Mr. Bohn for the purpose. I gave the MS. to him, and he promised to consider it and communicate with her. After a time she informed me that she could get no answer of any sort from him, that the volume was published, and finally that she found her poem in it under his own name, with some trifling alterations. I called on Mr. Bohn for an explanation, and only met with a great deal of vehement wrath, and an absolute denial that he had used any of her poem. I then asked him to return the MS., but I did not succeed in getting it back. I can say no more of this transaction from my own knowledge, but I have never doubted that Speranza's statements were strictly accurate."

If Gavan Duffy had a good opinion of Speranza she for her part had an equally good one of him. "He was," she said, "a man of the highest culture, of exquisite literary taste, and a clever and powerful writer of both prose and verse. He was eminently fitted for guide and counsellor to all the young fiery intellects that composed his staff, while his winning manners and earnest sympathy with all that was noble and beautiful in literature and art gained him their admiration and love."

Altogether, an ideal editor.

CHAPTER 4

DOUBLE HARNESS

I

It was shortly after the suppression of The Nation that, when visiting some friends, Gavan Duffy's star contributor made the acquaintance of a young Dublin medical man, Dr. Wilde, in practice as an oculist. Much was to come of that chance meeting.

William Robert Wills Wilde, to give him his full name, may be said to have represented the fusion of the Saxon with the Celt. His Durham born grandfather, one Ralph Wilde, had settled in Ireland about the middle of the 18th century, where, establishing himself in Castlerea, County Roscommon, he married a Galway heiress, Miss O'Flynn. For a member of an English Protestant family to become the husband of the daughter of an Irish Papist was resented by the relatives of both parties, and severed all further intercourse between them. Of this marriage there were two sons, Ralph, a clergyman, and Thomas, a doctor, who, marrying a Miss Fynn, became in 1815, the father of William Robert Wilde. Through his wife he was connected with the families of Gideon Ouseley, distinguished as a missionary and scholar, W. G. Wills, the dramatist, and George Moore, the novelist.

Electing to adopt the same career as his father, it was in Dublin that young William Wilde began his medical studies by being apprenticed to a surgeon at Steevens's Hospital, where one of his contemporaries was Charles Lever. In addition to his work in the wards, he did yeoman service as a volunteer in combating the cholera epidemic that swept Ireland in the early 'thirties. From the outbreak of the scourge he was unceasing in his efforts to check its ravages, and attributed his own escape from becoming a victim to a plentiful consumption of brandy and porter. The prescription was followed in after years, and adhered to even when there was no longer any danger of infection. Fortunately, he had a strong head.

Having received his diploma in 1837, Dr. Wilde, anxious to gain further experience before setting up his brass plate, "walked" a London hospital. Devoting himself to aural and ophthalmic work, he continued his studies in Berlin, Paris, and Vienna. While in Vienna, he profited by attending lectures and operations at the Allgemeine Krankenhaus, the leading hospital and medical school in Austria. He also found time to go into society, and, having good introductions, was a constant guest at balls, receptions, soirées, and dinner-parties. Notwithstanding his uncouth and almost simian figure and features, he was—thanks, perhaps, to his Irish tongue and ever-ready supply of "blarney", on tap—a great success with women. Carrying off a stock of glowing testimonials from his professors, he returned to Dublin, where he established himself as a specialist in diseases of the eye and ear, and soon built up a large and remunerative practice.

T. M. Healy, K.C., when a young barrister, once had occasion to consult him. "He removed," he says, "a squint from the eye of a British princess when no one else would attempt the operation." But he was not so successful with a less exalted patient. This was the father of Bernard Shaw, whom he treated for obliquity of vision. As a result of the "cure" it is recorded that Shaw senior "squinted the other way all the rest of his life".

To his medical and surgical work Dr. Wilde added a cultivated taste for literature. This was developed early in his career. At the age of twenty-five he produced a *Narrative of a Voyage to Teneriffe*, for which an enterprising publisher paid him £250 and sold three thousand copies. This was followed by a scholarly memoir of Dean Swift,* in which a point was made of rebutting the attacks of Brougham and Jeffreys, and a number of volumes giving evidence of a sound knowledge of archaeology, biography, and natural history. Prominent among these were his *Beauties of the Boyne and Blackwater; Lough Corrib: its Shores and Islands; History of Irish Medicine; Irish Fairy Lore;* and a *Descriptive Catalogue of Irish Antiquities in the Royal Irish Academy.* This last work, filling three volumes, proved a laborious task. "Had I known," he wrote, "the amount of physical and mental labour I was to go through when I undertook the Catalogue, I would not have considered it just to myself to have done it, for I may fairly say it has been done at the risk of my life."

The first of the three volumes appeared in 1857, prefaced by a note from the President:

"The work of classifying and arranging the Museum, and also the preparation of the Catalogue, was gratuitously undertaken by Mr. Wilde, who has devoted his time and labour to the task with an energy and zeal which entitle him to the warmest thanks of the Academy."

---

* But for all his close study of Swift's works, Wilde once fell into a trap. This was in his account of a somewhat coarse satire purporting to have been written by a Drury Lane actress to a rival. Although the various names in it were invented by Swift, Wilde regarded them as referring to real persons and to be a reflection on the morals of the contemporary Dublin theatre.

It was as a result of these dual activities that
Dr. Wilde* was elected to the membership of various
learned societies, and also to the Presidency of the
Royal Irish Academy. But his name and fame soon
spread beyond Dublin; and, when he was still under
forty, he received a special honour, viz, an appointment as "Surgeon-Oculist-in-Ordinary" to the Queen.
It is true that her Majesty never had occasion to
consult him professionally. Still, as the man on the
spot, he would have been available for the purpose
should she have happened to require his treatment
when visiting Ireland.

2

Apart from their common interest in literature (in
after years they collaborated on two books, and also
in some articles they contributed jointly to the *Irish
Quarterly Review*, which was owned and edited by
Dr. Wilde) the two found that they shared other
tastes. As a result, the acquaintance between them
progressed rapidly; and in the winter of 1851, when
Wilde was thirty-six and Miss Elgee was just twenty-
five, their marriage took place. The ceremony, on
November 21, was conducted at St. Peter's Church
by the Rev. John Wilde, a relative of the bridegroom.
Several of his colleagues from Steevens's Hospital were
present to support him, but no members of the bride's
family followed their example. The reason for their
absence was probably that none of them lived within
easy reach of Dublin, and the condition of the country
roads made winter travelling difficult. Miss Elgee, by
the way, was not her husband's first choice, for he had

---

* An interesting study of William Wilde is *A Victorian Doctor*, by T. G
Wilson: Methuen.

once proposed to (and been refused by) Helen Faucit,
the well-known Shakespearian actress who afterwards
married Sir Theodore Martin.

To most observers the bridegroom and bride must
have appeared a somewhat ill-matched pair. William
Wilde, eleven years the elder of the two, was devoid
of any graces of feature or figure. He was under
average height, and, with his long shaven upper lip
and shambling walk, is said to have looked rather like
an overgrown ape. Miss Elgee, on the other hand,
was a well-built and attractive young woman, with
raven hair, dark flashing eyes, and an air of distinction.

A somewhat belated honeymoon was spent in
Scandinavia. This was not a country which, owing
to bad communications, was often selected for the
purpose by travellers from Ireland. It had, however,
been chosen by Dr. Wilde because the abundance
of pre-historic remains to be found there appealed to
his antiquarian and ethnological interests. A number
of letters of introduction to certain learned professors
with whom he had corresponded were procured, and
a stock of guide books packed in the couple's port-
manteaux.

All being in readiness for the expedition, they set off
from Dublin on the first stage of the trip.

"Behold us, then," says the young bride, "one
lovely August morning at the great hall door of the
world, Liverpool, *en route* for Copenhagen, via Hull,
Hamburg, and Kiel, the shortest and cheapest line of
travel. . . . Having heard that only sick people,
puppy dogs, and the English travelled first class, we
went second for the sake of the company."

The fellow-passengers were somewhat mixed, for on
board the steamer were "several Hull merchants, an

alligator, six monkeys, and half-a-dozen Germans, all bound for Berlin". The trip, however, was economical, as the fare was only two pounds a head. But it was recorded with sorrow that "an extra fifteen shillings a day was charged for meals". Still, since ten substantial repasts were provided by the purser, the tariff was not really extortionate.

The first stopping-place was Kiel, where the voyagers transhipped for Copenhagen. After exploring the city (not forgetting to sample the Tivoli Gardens and the cafés) Mrs. Wilde left with a good impression of the Danes. "The brutalities of lower-class English life are unknown amongst them," she said. "Yet," she added, "they are not much preached to. The religion of Denmark is simply homage to the beautiful; belief without dogma; and a gentlemanly repugnance to coarse and vulgar crime. Any bondage to a priesthood would be looked upon as mere cant of superstition."

From Copenhagen, the travellers went as far as Christiania and Stockholm, where they inspected museums and picture galleries, and attended numerous banquets held in their honour. During their stay in Sweden they were the guests of Baron von Kroemar, the Viceroy of Uppsala, who acted as their cicerone. A distinction between the three countries was noted by the observant Mrs. Wilde. "The Norse," she remarked, "are democrats, the Swedes courtiers, and the Danes artistic Bohemians. Soil and climate have created the national character . . . In Sweden one thinks of history and heroes."

Leaving Scandinavia, a short stop in Berlin was made on the way home. Mrs. Wilde was not favourably impressed with this part of the trip. Thus, "the Customs officials were rude and resolute";

"there was no beauty among the women", and, "what can be done with a globular mass of formless features?" Still, she had a good word for German actors and actresses! "They act with intellect, and as if entirely one with the author, whose lines they utter, and whose spirit they interpret."

She also had something to say about a parade of the garrison she attended at Potsdam:

"The military have more pretension and style than any other class of the people. The young officers are a fine race, but whether their breadth of shoulder, convexity of chest, and tenuity of waist is due to Nature or the tailor I cannot determine. The erect military bearing and firm step of the Prussian contrasts wonderfully with the shambling, shuffling gait of the French soldier, who has no more form or firmness than the knapsack he carries."

After this, a somewhat rash prophecy was announced:

"The Slav will never conquer the Teuton. Neither will the French ever succeed in a war of reprisal or revenge. They need not attempt it." To this she added: "The Germans, who live on beer and cheese, are not, and never can be, politically dangerous ".

All things considered, perhaps it was as well that there were no more of these assumptions of the rôle of a Cassandra.

3

On returning to Dublin, Dr. Wilde brought back with him an *honoris causa* degree from the University of Uppsala, the Order of the Polar Star of Sweden, and notes for a lecture to be delivered by him to the members of the Royal Irish Academy. Nor did his

bride return empty-handed, as she had amassed
material for her first published book, *The Glacier Land*,
as well as for a number of poems. Among these was
one which, translated from the Danish, began :

> For Norway, Freedom's fatherland,
> Fill up the wine-cup flowing,
> And pledge it, brothers, hand in hand,
> To keep the hot blood glowing.
>
> By gyves and fetters rent we swear
> No tyrant's hand shall ever dare
> To chain our souls while swords we bear
> To guard old Norway's freedom !

A reporter, instructed to "do the books" for a local
paper, described this effort as a "sonnet".

"He probably didn't know any better," was
Speranza's comment.

The first Dublin residence of Dr. and Mrs. Wilde
was at No. 15 Westland Row. They soon, however,
moved further up the same street to No. 21. After a
couple of years there the doctor's increasing practice
made it possible to take a larger house in a superior
quarter. This was No. 1 Merrion Square, a good
example of the Georgian architecture that characterized Dublin at that date. For neighbours there
were judges and lawyers, leading representatives of
Trinity College, and heads of the medical profession.
The rooms were furnished in the approved style of
the period with heavy mahogany tables and chairs,
walnut cabinets and book cases, huge oil paintings by
"fashionable" artists, and an abundance of Turkey
carpets and rugs. There was also plenty of accom-
modation for entertaining; and Dr. Wilde saw to it that
there was always a well-stocked cellar.

Three children resulted from the marriage, two sons, Willie and Oscar, and a daughter, Isola, who died at the age of ten. Of these children, the eldest, born in 1852, was christened William, with Charles Kingsbury added as a makeweight, and his brother Oscar followed him in 1854. Their mother was then twenty-eight, and their father was thirty-nine.

The appearance of this new occupant of the nursery was notified by his mother in a characteristic letter to a friend.

"A Joan of Arc was never meant for marriage, and so here I am, bound heart and soul to the home hearth. Behold me, Speranza, rocking a cradle at this present writing in which lies my second son—a babe of one month old the 16th of this month, November, and as large and fine and handsome and healthy as if he were three months.   He is to be called Oscar Fingal Wilde. Is not that grand, misty, and Ossianic?"

When, as a young man, he was staying at Avignon, Oscar, who had been much attached to his little sister, commemorated her death in a poem, *Requiescat*, which, if obviously reminiscent of another with a similar title by Matthew Arnold (and also one by Tom Hood) none the less touched a genuine chord of feeling.   The first two verses ran :

> Tread lightly, she is near
>   Under the snow,
> Speak gently, she can hear
>   The daisies grow.

> All her bright golden hair
>   Tarnished with rust,
> She that was young and fair
>   Fallen to dust.

In after years the author himself was not particularly impressed by this juvenilia. "I don't know that I think *Requiescat* very typical of my work," he wrote, when somebody wanted to include it in an anthology. Forty years later, however, the manuscript fetched £22 in a London sale room.

With typical extravagance, or else not content with Oscar by itself, when his parents took their infant son to the font and the officiating clergyman said, "Name this child", the response was, "Oscar Wills Fingal O'Flaherty". This was certainly a bit of a mouthful with which to saddle a youngster not old enough to utter an effective protest. Hence, it is not surprising that, on emerging from boyhood and in a position to choose for himself, he thought the first of this string enough for all practical purposes and dropped the last three names that had been bestowed on him.

"I am Oscar to my friends, and Mr. Wilde to everybody else," he would announce when desirous of checking undue familiarity on the part of strangers.

4

Early in the year 1855 Mrs. Wilde made the acquaintance of Sir William Rowan-Hamilton, the famous astronomer and mathematician. Robert Perceval Graves,* in his biography of him, has some interesting particulars of the close friendship that sprang up between the two:

"In the spring of the year," runs one passage, "Hamilton met, for the first time, Mrs. Wilde, afterwards Lady Wilde, the wife of Sir William R. Wilde, the eminent physician and Irish Archaeologist,

---

* *Life of Sir William Rowan-Hamilton:* R. P. Graves: Hodges Figgis and Co.

herself remarkable as a woman of warm feelings and literary faculty, shown in patriotic and eloquent contributions to newspapers and other less ephemerical periodicals, and in poems published under the name of *Speranza*, and, it may be truly added, as a woman of high aspirations and real genius. The acquaintance rapidly ripened into friendship, and a correspondence ensued in which Hamilton sometimes acted as critic of a poem by *Speranza*, and at other times confided to her the story of his life."

Hamilton himself gives an account of this first meeting in a letter to a fellow mathematician, Augustus de Morgan :

May 4, 1855.

A very odd and original lady, entirely unlike the one to whom I have been last alluding, had also lately a baby; such things, you know, will happen, at least in Ireland; and on my being asked to hand her in to dinner at a party given by Colonel and Mrs. Larcom in this neighbourhood, when I met her for the first time in my life, she told me of this "young pagan" as she called him (or it, for I did not know the sex) and she asked me to be godfather, perhaps because I was so to a grandson of Wordsworth, and because she is an admirer of Wordsworth. However, I declined. But it seems I have not fallen entirely out of favour thereby, for she paid me on Saturday last a visit of three hours and a half, it being my *second* time of seeing her . . . My visitress told me, as we drank a glass of wine to the health of her child, that he had been christened on the previous day by a long baptismal name, or string of names, the first two of which are Oscar and Fingal ! the third and fourth sounding to *me* as a tremendous descent, but I daresay she prefers them.

You must know that I have long been acquainted with her husband, as a member of the Royal Irish Academy, though he had not time to come with his wife on her long and entertaining visit of the other day. She is quite a genius, and thoroughly aware of it.

Anxious to have her new friend's critical opinion, Mrs. Wilde sent him one of her poems, *Shadows from Life*. The first two verses ran :

I

Vain the love that looketh upward, we may worship, adore;
From the heart's o'erflowing chalice all the tide of feeling pour;
Dash our souls against the barriers that divide us from the shrine;
Fling the incense; pour libations—aye, of life's own ruddy wine;
But the angel we gaze up to, calm as form of pictured saint,
From its golden mist of glory bendeth never to our plaint;
Heedeth not if crushed the temple where the altar fires burned,
For the doom runs through the ages—Love was never yet returned.

II

Thus it was he loved a lady; never priest in Aspahan
So adored when mount and ocean morning's flashing glories span.
Never sun-god in its glory, marching stately from the east,

Crimson-robed and cloud-attended, heeded less the
　　praying priest,
Then the lady, that pale lover, while her lonely path
　　she took
O'er the spirit's glittering summits, with her proud
　　and queenly look;
Like that Roman Sybil bearing in her hands the
　　mystic scroll,
And her large eyes looking onward where the future
　　ages roll.

Sir William Hamilton had a high opinion of
Shadows from Life. He told the author he found it
"wonderfully beautiful", but, struck by the liberties
taken with the metre, he added : "The metre seems to
change, as scanned, in the last few lines; yet, to my
ear, it has a pleasing effect". Less generous critics
who pointed out that the metre was obviously copied
from *Locksley Hall* forgot that it had been adopted
often enough by others long before Tennyson.

The few alterations suggested by Sir William were
received in such good part that he wrote to express his
thanks :

Dear Mrs. Wilde,

You have perfectly astounded me by your
patience and good humour, shown in not merely
tolerating, but adopting, my criticisms, or some of
them, on your very beautiful verses. I long to
spare time enough to write out the whole of that
poem, 'Shadows from Life', with those minor modi-
fications which have occurred to me here and there.

Apparently he did find time to do this; and his friend
Aubrey de Vere, to whom he sent a copy, declared
himself much impressed and wrote to Hamilton :

Mount Trenchard, December 20, 1855

Talking of poetry puts me in mind of your fair friend. . . . She certainly must be a woman of real poetic genius to have written anything so beautiful, and also so full of power and grace as the poem you showed me. For the sake both of poetry and Old Ireland you must do all you can to make her go on writing, and publish a volume soon. Do not forget to tell her that you showed her poem to a stranger (a stranger always counts for something) who has been addicted to poetry* all his life, and reveres it more every year, and that he has felt a very sincere admiration for it; although in the matter of your proposed metrical changes he had the impertinence to agree with *you*.

When this was reported to her, Mrs. Wilde registered gratification at the compliment. Thereupon, de Vere wrote to Hamilton :

I send you back Speranza's most amiable letter. It is indeed pleasant to meet that rare thing, poetic genius in union with a rarer one—the magnanimity (in which genius is so often deficient, and without which it almost ceases to be respectable) which can take censure with gratitude, praise with simplicity, and both with equal grace.

Thinking they would have much in common, Sir William, anxious to bring them together, tried to arrange a meeting between the two. It did not, however, materialize, for when Aubrey de Vere called on her with a letter of introduction, Speranza was in

---

* Aubrey de Vere's own poems were said to be "too intellectual to become popular", and towards the end he had to bear the cost of publication himself. He once jestingly said, "If I ceased to write poetry my income would be doubled".

the country, accompanied by her husband and children.

In the letter to his friend Aubrey de Vere, when he wanted him to meet Speranza, Hamilton wrote:

> She is the wife of an eminent surgeon, W. R. Wilde, Esqre . . . She is undoubtedly a genius herself, and she won my heart very soon . . . She is almost amusingly fearless and original, and averse (though in that, as in other respects) she perhaps exaggerates whatever is unusual about her that she likes to make a *sensation* . . . I think she has a noble nature (though a rebellious one).

In the summer of 1858 Aubrey de Vere wrote to his friend from Torquay, lamenting that he had missed him in Dublin:

> Nor was I more fortunate as regards your friend Speranza, at whose house I called in vain. I sent her also my Search after *Proserpine*, and *Misdeeds* (as some of my English friends call my vindication of Ireland) but I do not know whether they ever reached her. So, when you next meet her, pray tell her that the books were sent.

This letter crossed one which Hamilton had written to Mrs. Wilde:

> I am unable to recall—so much of human music was there in the poetical party at which you were so kind as lately to assist . . . May I pass abruptly to a quite different subject, and express a hope that Aubrey de Vere will not succeed in converting, or in perverting you.

Sir William's letters, carefully preserved, were read and re-read by their recipient. One of the earliest of the series ran:

After having known, so long and so intimately, another female genius, it is not perhaps extravagant to imagine that I may understand you, even on a very recent introduction, better than crowds of persons who may, by a longer acquaintance, be entitled to pay you a much greater degree of attention.

The further correspondence with Speranza, which is reproduced here by permission of Sir Sidney Orme Rowan-Hamilton, was maintained for a considerable period. It was Sir William, however, who seems to have written most of the letters. One from him, after a visit he had received from her, ran :

You must know that Lady Hamilton has been growing very jealous about you—not in the sense which might first occur to a sentimental schoolgirl. She did not at all think that I had paid too much attention to you—but after hearing me talk so much about you, and knowing that you had paid me a long (though not by any means a *too* long) visit, and that I had afterwards sent you my book with an inscription, she asked me about twenty times, "Why does not Mrs. Wilde write you a line?" "Why," I said, "I have not written a line to her. It was to her husband I wrote"; and perhaps she thinks that I ought to have had the civility to call upon her since her visit here. She is an authoress besides, and may be deeply engaged.

The next day Sir William sent her another letter :

Dear Mrs. Wilde, I did not fail to lay your gracious and graceful letter before my wife, as soon as she was awake this morning, and she read it and was much gratified by it.

Anxious to see more of his friend's work, he wrote:

It has been a pleasure to me to write so freely to a poetess. If you be a bit of a rebel also, tho' I am none, let not that prevent you from allowing me to see anything which you have printed, or from telling me where I can see it.

Speranza's response was expressed in terms that attracted another letter from her correspondent:

Observatory, February 11, 1858

You know whatever it may be at any time your pleasure to say, even if it be in praise of myself, I submit to it from the profound conviction felt by me of your being an entirely truthful person.

Of course it is needless to say that I am not to be considered as adopting any expression which it would not have been modest in *me* to have first uttered, but to which I have (once or twice) listened, without remonstrance from you—for the reason mentioned above.

It may not sound very consistent with any such professional humility on my part if I say to you that, after having served for the Quarternions during fourteen years, and having (as America seems to think) won my Rachel—to be my own by an intellectual marriage—I now wish to wind up several scientific projects, from which those quarternions had for a long time diverted me; and feel as if I were entering, or had already entered, on a new harvest of labour and reputation. As to *Fame*, if it has not been won or earned already, it is not likely that any future exertion will make it mine.

5

Sir William Hamilton's interest in poetry was
largely due to the fact that, in addition to being more
—a good deal more—than something of a poet himself
(as evidenced by the fact that on two occasions he had
been awarded the Vice-Chancellor's prize for English
verse at Trinity College) his favourite sister, Eliza, was,
as a young girl, the author of many admirable lyrics
and ballads. Speranza, who had expressed warm
enthusiasm for them, received from Sir William a copy
of his sister's published volume in which he had written,
"Presented to Mrs. Wilde with the affectionate regards
of one who has been gratified by her kind appreciation
of the poetical genius of his departed sister".

In one of her many letters to him Speranza wrote :

I am never happier than with such thoughts as
you send me in all forms. Sometimes they bring
tears, sometimes strength. I never "tire" of what
ministers to the mental life—believe this, even if I am
ungracious enough to have unacknowledged the gold,
frankincense, and myrrh you send me.

This, and a similar communication that followed it,
brought a characteristically modest response :

My correspondents know that, as a rule, I do not
like them to write a single word of praise; but
everything you write appears so good and natural
that I cannot find it in my heart to blame you for
expressing your too favourable estimate of me.

R. P. Graves, who was very intimate with him, says
that although he liked praise, Hamilton also feared it
if overdone. Since, too, he felt that reciprocal
admiration might degenerate into reciprocal flattery,
one of Mrs. Wilde's letters attracted this response :

. . . At all events you are no *chaplain* of mine, but only a fair *compatriot*, whose Irish feelings prompt you to take the most favourable view in your power of one who is essentially an Irishman by birth, and life and labour, though educated by a clergyman who held the ascendancy principles (from which by very slow degrees I have been through life gradually emancipating myself), and who would have regarded repeal as rebellion. It was English history, not Irish, which I was taught; and my heart still throbs with sympathy for that great British Empire to which from childhood I have been accustomed to consider myself as belonging— though Ireland, as Ireland, has always been the object of my *love*—and, I think you will admit, of my exertions. God forbid, then, that I should even smile, and I pray you also not to think it, at any grief or sadness or depression which any feeling of patriotism may have caused you. Education has much to do with the direction of such a feeling; but I know what it is, without hope or fear of any private gain or loss, to sympathize with a *nation*. I was almost sick with sorrow at hearing of the disasters in Cabool and the Khyber Pass several years ago.

Interested in her domestic life, he added :

I congratulate you, as a woman of genius, on being so happily married (which my sister never was) and on having such fine children.

He remembered their full names, for a postscript ran : "Not forgetting William Charles Kingsbury, nor Oscar Fingal O'Flaherty"; and an entry in his "Daybook", after a visit to Westland Row, records : "I saw Willie, and gave him a little sixpenny roll of comfits". Although not sharing them to the full, Hamilton had abundant sympathy with Speranza's political views. "I believe," he wrote, "that such a genius is never more a woman than when she seems in some excited moment to beat her breast against the bars of some imprisoning cage of society."

Speranza had spoken warmly of a book that had impressed her. This extracted a response: "I have read more than once, since you mentioned it to me, 'The Scarlet Letter' of Hawthorne. The passion, the stress of human agony, expressed or hinted at in that book is indeed tremendous. If it did not actually cost me 'three nights' sleep', which I think was your own estimate, and which I was all the time amused by your mentioning as a recommendation of the book to me, who lose so many hours of natural rest by study, it has certainly stood between me and many hours of other reading or writing."

To us it seems incredible, but in those mid-Victorian days anything suggesting a married man's interest in another woman was apt to be frowned upon by the censorious. Aware of this, perhaps, Hamilton added in one of his last letters: "Of course I could never presume to imagine that anything I may at any time write to you will not be shown to Dr. Wilde. . . . I believe, and have satisfaction in believing, that he will, as fully as you, respect any confidence which may be implied in the very fact of any such letters as these".

In April, 1858, the friendship between the two had so far developed that Sir William could write:

Can I do better, or more pleasantly, commemorate our first meeting, which occurred exactly three years ago, on the 13th of April, 1855, at the hospitable house of Colonel* and Mrs. Larcom,

* Colonel Thomas Larcom, Royal Engineers, attached to the Ordnance Department in Dublin.

than by introducing you to my old and dear
(I regret that I am obliged to add my Popish) friend,
Aubrey de Vere, the poet and prose writer, with
some of whose principal work in prose you are
already acquainted?

But something always happened to prevent it, and
the two did not meet again.

As time crept on, other interests would appear to
have occupied them, and Hamilton's letters became
less frequent and gradually ceased. The last one he
wrote to Speranza was in April, 1861, when he sent
her a gossiping account of a visit he had paid to
Cambridge.

"It would be unnecessary," adds R. P. Graves in
his account of the correspondence between the two,
"to leave unrecorded the fact that Hamilton was not
only interested in the mind of this gifted country-
woman, but esteemed highly her whole nature, in
which he recognized many features of native nobility."

CHAPTER 5

DUBLIN DAYS

I

MATRIMONY and motherhood did not check Mrs. Wilde's literary ambitions. If anything, indeed, they acted as an incentive to still greater activity; and in 1863 she was starred as "one of the principal contributors to Duffy's *Hibernian Magazine*". This was a sixpenny monthly for which she wrote a number of poems and essays, signed Speranza, a *nom de guerre* to which she adhered throughout the remainder of her career.

"Except to the poet," lamented John Davidson, "the age of poetry is always dead." But it was never dead to Speranza. Having once lit the lamp, she made it her unceasing care to keep it alight and trimmed; and, setting to work to collect a number of her stray efforts, she soon had enough for a volume. In 1864 this was published by a Dublin firm as *Poems by Speranza*, with a prefatory note, "Dedicated to my sons, Willie and Oscar". This note, however, was omitted from the second edition which was afterwards issued in Glasgow.

Some of the contents of this volume made their first appearance in print. Others had already been published in the columns of THE NATION and the *Hibernian Magazine*; and one of them, "A Lament for the Potato" (which met with Swinburne's approval) was extracted from the *Dublin University Magazine*.

In one of the poems, "The Fall of the Tyrants", the influence of Macaulay was clearly visible:

Ho! Spaniards! rise for liberty—
Your country on ye calls,
To fight today, in proud array
Before Granada's walls;
A proud array is here today,
Full fifty thousand strong,
Of Fantassins and Coralins
Gonzalo leads along.

But there were also echoes of Eliza Cook and Adah Isaacs Menken in other efforts; and some of them would appear to have been inspired by Letitia Landon and Mrs. Norton.

Speranza, however, had a great opinion of her attempts to surmount the heights of Parnassus.

"You and other poets," she once informed a friend, "are content to express only your own little soul in poetry. I express the soul of a great nation. Nothing less would satisfy me, who am the acknowledged voice in poetry of all the people of Ireland."

Although she is omitted from Lennox Robinson's *Golden Treasury of Irish Verse*, as also from W. B. Yeats's *Book of Irish Verse*, Speranza is accorded a place of honour in a number of less exigently compiled anthologies. Among such are Stopford Brooke's *Treasury of Irish Poetry*, John Cook's *Dublin Book of Irish Verse*, Edward Hayes' *Ballads of Ireland*, Martin MacDermott's *New Spirit of the Nation*, and Charles Read's *Cabinet of Irish Literature*. Further, John Boyle O'Reilly, in his *Poetry and Songs of Ireland*, says of her output: "In the stormy days of 'Young Ireland', from 1846-48, the poems of Speranza, next to those of Thomas Davis, were the inspiration of the National Movement".

SIR WILLIAM WILDE

SIR WILLIAM AND LADY WILDE

Sketch by HARRY FURNISS

2

A certain January morning in 1864 was a red-letter day in the Merrion Square household, for on the 28th of that month Dr. Wilde was summoned to attend a Chapter of the Knights of St. Patrick at Dublin Castle. There, dropping on one knee, he received the accolade and was commanded by Lord Carlisle, the Viceroy, to "Rise, Sir William." In so doing, His Excellency improved the occasion by announcing : "The honour of knighthood is conferred on you, not so much in recognition of your professional skill, which is European, as in recognition of the distinguished services you have rendered to statistical science, especially in connection with the preparation of the Irish Census Report". As Robert Sherard shrewdly points out, this latter reason had a touch of official cynicism about it, for, wrapped up in the body of the Report, was a good deal that was anything but complimentary to the Castle authorities. In fact, it rated them soundly for their systematic neglect of their duties.

Although in days gone by she had employed her pen to voice a desire to "burn down Dublin Castle", to "push out the English garrison", to "cause the British Throne to totter", and generally upset things, Speranza was as pleased as Punch to become "her Ladyship"; to have her portrait, painted by Bernard Mulrenin, exhibited at the Royal Hibernian Academy Exhibition of 1864, and to attend His Excellency's drawing-rooms. The link-man's warning, "Lady Wilde's carriage stops the way!" was as music to her ears. Snobbish, perhaps. Still, we all have our little weaknesses; and Lady Wilde was none the worse for hers.

The knighthood was generally approved by the

Dublin press. "Need we say," enquired a smug journalist, "what satisfaction it affords us to congratulate Lady Wilde on the honour which has been bestowed on her eminent husband? Need we add that Speranza also has many claims to the respect of her country such as no Queen or Viceroy could confer. Ireland, indeed, has good reason to be proud of Lady Wilde; and we do not hesitate to assert that she is at the present moment the most popular lady in the land of her birth, and the most highly gifted one wherever the English language is read or spoken."

Compliments also for her husband. "Sir William Wilde has many claims to the distinction of the accolade just conferred on him," declared the *Lancet*. "He has taken part in three successive censuses of Ireland, and is also known by his erudite antiquarian studies, which have won for him a considerable reputation as an accomplished archaeologist. We congratulate the Irish profession on the honour bestowed on one of its most distinguished representatives."

The *British Medical Journal* also offered compliments: "We congratulate Sir William Wilde on his new dignity, and the medical profession in Ireland on the circumstance that it has been conferred on so worthy a member of their body".

By the way, in the particulars relating to himself, as published in the "Court Guide" portion of the Dublin Directory, the descriptive note for several years following the bestowal of the knighthood repeated the old error : "Married Jane Francesca, daughter of the late Archdeacon Elgee". It would seem, therefore, that proofs of this entry had not been submitted to, nor corrected by, Sir William. Otherwise, he would certainly not have passed it.

Now that he had a "handle to his name", Sir William was soon in demand for public appearances. One invitation that he accepted was, supported by the presence of the Dean of the Chapel Royal in the Chair, to lecture to the Dublin branch of the Young Men's Christian Association on "Ireland, Past and Present". He was in good company, for the other lecturers secured by the Committee included the Archbishop of Dublin, Lord Dufferin, the Rev. A. K. H. Boyd, and Samuel Warren. He also read a paper to the Anthropological Section of the British Association when that learned body held its 1874 meeting in Belfast. This was afterwards printed as a pamphlet.

A Dublin weekly, *Zozimus*, a feeble imitation of *Punch*, published a caricature, labelled "The Cur-Eye-Ous Knight". Appended to this effort were some verses, one of which ran :

Our Knight, more bold, his trusty weapon sets
    Against the cataract, and though he wins
He wins not as the knights of old, he lets
    Not "daylights" out, but daylight in!

According to the editorial pronouncement, the particular object of *Zozimus* was "to bring home amusement to all, and to spread around the merry laugh, uninfluenced by the social or political views of its constituents". There was, however, very little in its pages to suggest that this result was secured. As a consequence *Zozimus* expired with the second volume.

3

In addition to enjoying a substantial income from his surgical practice, Sir William Wilde derived a second (but much smaller) one from some property he owned in County Mayo. He was a popular landlord, and never allowed his tenants to be unduly pressed when times were hard, nor shut his ears to a genuine tale of misfortune.

But large as was his professional income, it was not large enough to balance his personal budget. At No. 1 Merrion Square it was a case of "easy come, easy go". Everything there was conducted on an extravagant scale. Open house was the rule; a score of hangers-on (half of them as often as not self-invited) sat down to luncheon and dinner and supper every day. All comers received a hearty welcome; and, taking advantage of this, chance acquaintances would occupy the spare rooms for weeks on end, enjoying free board and lodgings, with lashings of drink. It was there, too, that Lady Wilde conducted what she fondly imagined was a *salon*. But, as her son Oscar said of somebody else, "she only succeeded in opening a restaurant".

"The house," says a visitor, "was a rallying place for all who were eminent in science, art, or literature. Dr. Shaw, the versatile sarcastic Fellow of Trinity College and a brilliant writer, was frequently seen there on Saturday afternoons; the 'Sham Squire', Mr. H. J. Fitzpatrick, the well-known biographer, seldom failed to show his melancholy aristocratic face; Dr. Tisdall gave some of his delightful and mirth-inspiring recitations; and Sir Robert Stewart often brightened the rooms with his cheery presence."

A constant visitor to No. 1 Merrion Square was Professor Mahaffy, afterwards Provost of Trinity College, and a Greek scholar of European reputation. Although he happened to be in Orders, he was a pronounced sceptic and made a point of dropping the prefix Reverend. A snob of the first water, he assiduously cultivated the "Castle set" and anybody who was included in it. As a monologist, nobody in Dublin (nor for that matter anywhere else) could talk him down; and in this capacity his flow, once started, would be almost a non-stop performance. With the idea of instructing the less expert, he wrote a manual on the "Art of Conversation". Lady Wilde, who received a presentation copy from him, was asked her opinion.

"I think," she said, "that you should have written it in Greek. Scholars would then understand it. My son Oscar tells me that you are familiar with the language."

But Mahaffy was not easily deflated, for his opinion of himself rendered him impervious to snubs. Yet, "with all his faults", says Boris Brazol,* "Mahaffy was endowed with a delicate instinct for the genius of classicism".

A chance guest at a typical Merrion Square reception would have wondered where he had penetrated. The rooms, lit by lamps and candles, were shuttered and closely curtained even in the afternoon when the sun was shining out of doors. People would be arriving and leaving continually, and filling the crowded rooms to overflowing. The assembly was always a curious one. With true Irish hospitality, everybody and anybody, so long as he (or she) could contribute to the interest of the gathering and had something to say, was made welcome.

"Bohemians preferred" might almost have been on the invitation cards sent out for the Merrion Square gatherings. Hence, the rooms would be thronged with a mixture of artists, barristers, dramatists, journalists, medical students, undergraduates from

---

* *Oscar Wilde:* Boris Brazol: Williams and Norgate.

Trinity College, and dashing young sparks from the Dublin garrison with a sprinkling of attractive colleens to keep their hostess in countenance. Not that such help was wanted by her, for she would listen to the flood of bawdy talk and lewd jests without turning a hair. In fact, she herself was not above contributing comments that, in more rigid circles would have met with criticism. But the Merrion Square chatelaine obviously shared Walpole's opinion and approved "bawdy talk since everybody present could join in it".

The hostess certainly made no attempt to check such talk. "We live in a bad prosaic age, but not in an age of good prose," was one of her aphorisms. Oscar, who chanced to overhear it, afterwards served it up as his own, but in a more elaborate form.

In this connection Bram Stoker records an example of a remark she made when she was introduced by him to a girl he described as "half English and half Irish".

"Glad to meet you, my dear," was the affable response. "Your English half is as welcome as your Irish bottom."

Again, when somebody wanted to bring to Merrion Square a certain young woman, on the ground that she was "respectable", a reproof was administered.

"You must never employ that description in this house. Only tradespeople are 'respectable'."

Altogether, a curious atmosphere in which to bring up a couple of small boys, who listened all ears to everything that was said.

That the hostess knew how to put her foot down when a guest threatened to monopolise the conversation is clear from an account by a visitor of a happening at a typical reception:

"One afternoon an elderly gentleman was descanting on his favourite hobby—the anti-vivisection movement. He droned on and on, and we yawned helplessly. Lady Wilde's eagle eye took in the situation at a glance. 'My dear Mr. So-and-so,' she exclaimed, with one of her most captivating smiles, 'do excuse me for interrupting you, but Miss X is going to give us a recitation, *The Bishop and the Caterpillar*, and we all want to hear it '."

Another of Speranza's remarks, pounced upon by Havelock Ellis, supplies a specimen of her characteristic habit of ignoring certain views held in more rigid circles. The subject under discussion at the moment was one that has a special appeal for present-day psychologists:—"There never," she said, "has been a woman yet in this world who wouldn't have given the top off the milk jug to some man if she had met the right one."

Speranza's greeting to the daughter of a third rate novelist was characteristic :

"Welcome, my dear. You resemble your intellectual father, but you do not have his noble brow. Still, I see from the form of your eyelids that you have marked artistic qualities . . . I hear you have a lover. This is a pity, since love puts an end to ambition. But don't on any account bind yourself until you have seen more of men."

But the subject of this warning did not act on the suggestion. "My fiancé," she says, "called nearly every day to see me. Lady Wilde had an interview with him. She recommended an elopement as being more romantic, and promised to help us in every way. I recollect her saying that my lover, 'though well-informed, was not brilliant, and that men do not require information so much as inspiration '."

This sounds the sort of thing Oscar might have said.

When she considered it required, Speranza's criticism could be caustic. Thus, on one occasion she said to an ambitious poet-taster who asked her opinion of something he had written : "Your sonnet is entitled 'To Posterity', but I doubt if it will reach that address".

Oscar could have told her that Voltaire had said this first.

4

Although both their parents were Protestants, a theory advanced by interested parties asserts that their two boys were brought up as Roman Catholics. An Irish Priest, Father Fox, in charge of a parish near Dublin, has an oblique reference to this matter in an article he contributed to a Boston magazine :

> When stationed at the reformatory I sometimes called on Sir William Wilde, who was reputed to be one of the cleverest oculists of his time. He was bitterly opposed to reformatories, and made no secret of his animosity; not so, however, his talented and patriotic wife, Lady Wilde, who was better known by her *nom de plume*, Speranza. She used to take lodgings every summer for herself and her children at a farm house, at the foot of the vale of Glencree, belonging to a worthy family of the name of Evans, intimate friends of mine. On my calling there one day she asked my permission to bring her children to our chapel to assist at Mass on Sundays. As we had a tribune in the chapel from which the boys and the altar could be seen without actual communication I readily acceded to her request, and after the Mass was over, I enjoyed many a pleasant hour with this excellent lady. I am not

sure whether she ever became a Catholic herself, but it was not long before she asked me to instruct two of her children, one of them being that future erratic genius, Oscar Wilde. After a few weeks I baptized these two children, Lady Wilde herself being present on the occasion. At her request I called on their father and told him what I had done, his sole remark being that he did not care what they were so long as they became as good as their mother.

So much for the theory. It would, however, appear to have been exploded when Boris Brazol, a recent biographer of Oscar Wilde, took the trouble to communicate on the subject with the Archbishop of Dublin. The answer he received to his question ran: "Enquiries have been made, and there is no record or tradition in Glencree or district that Oscar Wilde was baptized a Catholic there".

"It is only right to say," remarked one of the circle, James Glover, "that Lady Wilde always had a premonitory confidence in Oscar's superiority as against that of his elder brother. Visiting them one day at their house in Merrion Square, the late George Henry Moore—the father of George Moore—an earnest politician in the 'fifties and sixties', enquired of their mother what she thought of the two boys' prospects. 'Oh,' said Lady Wilde, 'Willie is all right—he has a first-class brain—but as for Oscar, he will turn out something wonderful.' " The fashion, however, in which he did eventually "turn out" was very far from what she could have imagined.

Of the Merrion Square *ménage* when Speranza (as Lady Wilde preferred to be known) queened it there and dispensed hospitality to all and sundry, Sobersides of the *Athenaeum* registered shocked disapproval. "Gathered at her hospitable table," he recorded, "would be found all manner of men—actors, artists, professors, divines—from whom prudish Dublin had hitherto kept carefully apart. Here was the first, and for a long time, the only 'Bohemian' house in Dublin."

Where this matter is concerned, Lord Alfred Douglas, in his *Oscar Wilde; A summing up*, gives an interesting picture of the Merrion Square *salon* as it was conducted in those now far-off days:*

"Here high thinking did not go hand in hand with plain living. The house was a hospitable one; it was a house of opulence and carouse; of late suppers and deep drinking; of careless talk and example. His (Oscar's) father's gallantries were the talk of Dublin. Even his mother, though a woman of spotless life and honour, had a loose way of talking which might have been a danger to her sons . . . The mother's *salon*, the father's supper-table, were frequented by boozy and boisterous Bohemians, than whom no city more than Dublin furnishes stranger specimens."

A lady journalist, in search of "copy", had a somewhat different opinion :

"Conspicuous among the distinguished throng gathered together on such occasions moved the tall figure of our hostess, inspiring and inspired"; and a masculine *confrère*, who was permitted to tuck his legs at times under the Merrion Square mahogany, wrote of them : "These reunions furnish one of the chief attractions of Dublin society, and are responsible for a gathering of the *élite*, privileged to listen to Speranza discussing literature and the arts."

But other subjects were also discussed.

---

* *Oscar Wilde: a Summing-up:* Lord Alfred Douglas: Duckworth and Co.

Being somewhat avid of publicity, and having a fondness for seeing her name and doings in the papers Lady Wilde took care that accounts of her *salon* should not be ignored by the press. Although "columnists" had not then come into being, gossiping paragraphs dealing with personalities were "featured" in the Dublin "society" organs; and journalists were made welcome at No. 1 Merrion Square and given lists of the guests. A typical report of one such gathering ran :

"On Saturday last Lady Wilde, who is everywhere accepted in Dublin as a second Madame Récamier, and whose literary work is recognized as being of the first importance, gave an 'At Home' at her residence in Merrion Square. Among the large and distinguished assembly could be observed leading members of the artistic, literary, musical and social worlds. Among them we noticed the Rev. Prebendary, J. P. Mahaffy and Professor Tyrrell and other members of the staff of Trinity College, and the editor of the *Dublin University Magazine*, with judges and barristers, civil servants and officials, two or three clergymen, and a contingent from the Theatre Royal and concert platform artistes fulfilling an engagement just now in Dublin. The conversation was, as might have been expected, of an elevating character, but the principal subject to be discussed was poetry. As our readers are aware, under her pseudonym Speranza, Lady Wilde has recently published a selection of her poems, a volume which has enjoyed a well-merited success. It was in its reference to volume that the *Dublin Review* remarked 'the contents have exerted a decided influence on all the intellectual and political activities of Young Ireland', and went on to declare that, 'great as may have been the influence of her character and conversation, Madame Roland has left us no example of her talent that will bear comparison with Lady Wilde's poems or prose '."

The success of the Merrion Square *salon* inspired feelings of envy among some of the habituées.

"How do you manage to get together such a lot of interesting people?" enquired a visitor.

"By interesting them," was the reply. "It's quite simple. All one has to do is to get all sorts of people —but no dull specimens—and take care to mix them. Don't trouble about their morals. It doesn't matter they haven't any."

"I know a famous newspaper correspondent in London. May I bring him to your next reception?"

"By all means. Still, a co-respondent would be a bigger draw. See if you can't get one."

Speranza's spouse was not often seen in the drawing-room during the progress of a reception. He much preferred to slip away to his study downstairs with some of his medical friends, and there, over whisky and cigars, discuss the latest Dublin gossip and scandal. That his own actions were responsible for some of it was common knowledge. Nor did it trouble him. "All work and no play," he would tell his listeners, "makes Jack a dull boy."

"Also a 'Wild(e) boy'," remarked an admiring colleague.

5

In his description of the personal appearance of the chatelaine of the Merrion Square household a frequenter* has written : "Her white-powdered blue-

---

* *Celebrities and I:* Henriette Corkran: Hutchinson.

black head was invariably crowned with a gilded laurel wreath, and her bosom and dress were always over-decorated with a collection of cheap, yet thoroughly artistic, jewellery."*

Out of feminine curiosity as much as anything else, a Miss Henrietta Corkran once attended a typical reception. "I have never, before or since", she wrote, "met anyone in the least like Lady Wilde. Altogether, she struck me as an odd mixture of nonsense, with a sprinkling of genius."

In describing her hostess, Miss Corkran's touch was just a little cattish:

"A very tall woman, she looked over six feet high. She wore that day a long crimson silk gown which swept the floor. Her skirt was voluminous; underneath it there must have been two crinolines, for, when she walked, there was a peculiar swaying, swelling movement like that of a vessel at sea, the sails filled with wind. Over the crimson were flounces of Limerick lace, and, round what had once been her waist, an Oriental scarf, embroidered with gold, was twisted. Her long, massive handsome face was plastered with white powder; and over her blue-black glossy hair was a crown of laurels. Her throat was bare, so were her arms, but they were covered with quaint jewellery. On her broad chest were fastened a series of large brooches, evidently family portraits, which came down almost as low as the gastronomical region, and gave her the appearance of a perambulating family mausoleum."

After this, it is not remarkable to learn that such a vision struck its recipient as "resembling a tragedy queen at a suburban theatre".

---

* " Lady Wilde," says Lord Rathcreedan, "was in the habit of wearing a red shawl."

This view is supported by a masculine critic, Harry Furniss.* "Lady Wilde", he says, "was a very tall and stoutishly inclined woman, with the appearance and air of a tragedy queen of the Mrs. Crummles type. She might have walked out of the pages of *Nicholas Nickleby*."

Yet, if a portrait of her that was painted in 1863 by Bernard Mulrenin of the Royal Irish Academy, is to be trusted, Speranza at this period suggested nothing of the kind. After all, she was only thirty-seven when the Merrion Square *salon* was in full swing.

A more sympathetic allusion to her admitted eccentricities was that of another visitor, the Comtesse de Brémont:

"What mattered the old-fashioned brocade gown, the long gold earrings, or the yellow lace fichu crossed on her breast and fastened with innumerable enormous brooches, the huge bracelets of turquoise and gold, and the rings on every finger? Her faded splendour was more striking than the most fashionable attire, for she wore that ancient finery with a grace and dignity that robbed it of its grotesqueness."

By the way, one of Speranza's guests, who was to distinguish himself above all the others, was Bernard Shaw. As a very young man he was taken to the *salon*. What impressed him about the company he encountered there was, as he wrote years afterwards to Ellen Terry, that it included Miss Glyn, the well-known Shakespearian actress who was playing in Dublin that week.

6

Although she affected a curious style of costume for

---

* *Some Victorian Women*: Harry Furniss: John Lane.

herself, Lady Wilde took an immense interest in feminine attire. An article which she contributed on the subject ran :

Dress ought to express a moral purpose. It symbolises the intellect. . . . The literary garb should be free, untrammelled and unswathed, and fastened only with a girdle or brooch. No stiff corselet should ever depress the full impulses of a passionate heart. There should be no false coils upon the head to weight upon the hair, no fuzzy bush on the brow to heat the temples and mar the cool logic of some grand deep thought. The fewer frills, cuffs, and cascades of lace the better. . . . Nothing to mind, nothing to care about, no bondage through fashion or vanity, either on soul or body, should be the law of dress for literary women. Certainly, no inspiration could have come to the Pythia had she worn a corselet and hoop. . . . Wives and mothers will always find it difficult to dress suitably for visits of inspection to the nursery and the kitchen, and at the same time elegantly enough to receive chance visitors in the drawing-room.

For afternoon receptions black should be sedulously avoided, either for the receiving or the received. Black is unlovely and unbecoming, especially to Englishwomen. Nothing can be more dreary at afternoon teas than rows of opaque black bundles along the walls of a drawing-room. . . . Englishwomen seem to have a fatal predisposition towards black. Perhaps the influence of Her Majesty has led to its general adoption in London. The Queen has never been seen by her subjects since her widowhood but as a mass of black dress,

bonnet, gloves and parasol all shrouded in the same
mysterious gloom. But the Queen is probably too
intellectual to pay much attention to dress.

In another passage the expert enlarged on this
subject:

A woman should study her own personality.
She should consider well what she means to be—
a superb Juno, a seductive Aphrodite, a blooming
Hebe, or a Pallas Athene. When the style that
suits her best—whether for homage or love—is
discovered, let her keep to it. As the symbol of her
higher self, unchanged by frivolous mutilations of
fashion, dress then attains a moral significance and
becomes the esoteric expression of the wearer's
spiritual nature.

Holding these sound views, it is a pity that Lady
Wilde did not always practise what she preached.

A young woman, whose mother was on intimate
terms with Lady Wilde at this period, says: "I had
often heard my family speak of Speranza as an
eccentric woman of genius, extravagant and even
foolish in language, holding absurd views about life".

Whatever her opinions about life, or, for that
matter, about anything else, Speranza was always
ready to lay down the law on them. As a conversationalist she enjoyed a certain repute. "Good
talk," she once observed, "is wasted on most people.
. . . Never be malicious, it is so vulgar. Epigram is
always better than argument in conversation, and
paradox is the very essence of social wit and brilliancy.
The unexpected, the strange combination of op-
posites, the daring subversion of some ancient plati-
tude, are all keen social weapons. But only assured
celebrity makes society pardon originality, for people

ISAAC BUTT, Q.C.
Counsel for Miss Travers

SIR WILLIAM ROWAN HAMILTON
Marble bust by FOLEY in the library of Trinity College Dublin

generally resent being suddenly lifted out of their old
grooves by the intellectual dynamite of some audacious
thinker and talker who has no respect for the laws of
social routine . . . Women, especially, must be aware
of originality. Unless therefore, their equals, clever
women should be vigilant to tone down their conversation to the regulation pattern. It is always safer
to begin with commonplaces. As for insignificant
people, they should only say what they are expected
to say. Anecdotes are best avoided. Nor should
conversation be allowed to condense into monologue at
a dinner-party."
Sound enough precepts, certainly. Still, not always
adhered to, even by Lady Wilde herself, who was
given to indulge in monologues.

7

As a result of the extravagant fashion in which the
household was conducted, poverty came in at the door
of No. 1 Merrion Square fairly often, with an accom-
panying barrage of duns and writs. Lady Wilde,
however, refused to be upset. Robert Sherard, who
knew her well, says that once, when a creditor, his
patience exhausted, put a couple of emissaries "in
possession", she consoled herself by reading Æschylus.
The philosophical temperament.
If Furniss was not effusively polite about the
chatelaine of No. 1 Merrion Square, he was less so
about her husband. "He resembled a monkey," was
his description of him, "a miserable-looking little
creature, who, apparently unshorn and unkempt,
looked as if he had been rolling in the dust."
"The heart is deceitful above all things," was the
sorrowful reflection of Jeremiah. A sad thought, yet
not altogether unfounded, for in the make-up of even

the best of us there are often warring and unamiable qualities. Sir William Wilde was no exception. Thus, grafted on to his undoubted culture and generous instincts ("for which many a poor Catholic priest had abundant cause to be thankful") was a less commendable trait. This was one of a strongly developed amorality. Having a "way with him", he was notorious for his gallantries. As he never attempted to conceal them, his amours and liaisons were the talk of Dublin; and it was perfectly well known that paternity could be attributed to him in respect of half-a-dozen children born on the wrong side of the blanket. Two of these were girls, and met with a tragic fate, being burned to death at a Christmas party.* With regard to the remainder, it is to his credit that he always acknowledged his responsibilities and provided for their support and education, setting up one of the brood as a doctor.

---

* In connection with this tragic occurrence a few years ago somebody wrote to an Irish paper, declaring that these girls were the daughters of Oscar Wilde, and that the writer of the letter had himself attended their funeral and seen "his tall figure standing beside the grave and weeping bitterly".

Well, Oscar was undoubtedly precocious, but at this date he was only a lad of sixteen. Consequently, the story may be discounted.

CHAPTER 6

CAUSE CÉLÈBRE

I

As everybody knows, the pitcher can go to the well too often; and it was one of the "gallantries" of Sir William Wilde that, in December, 1864, was nearly to prove the undoing of himself and his wife.

A few days before Christmas, the Dublin correspondent of a London paper wrote : "A trial which, on account of the social position of the parties concerned, has aroused among the public here a degree of interest surpassing even that of the recent Yelverton case, has been occupying the Court of Common Pleas all this week".

The action to which reference was thus made was listed as "Travers v. Wilde and Another". It was in respect of an alleged libel published by Lady Wilde; and the "Another" was her husband, who had been necessarily joined to the suit because he was in law responsible for her torts.

Miss Mary Josephine Travers, the plaintiff, was described by a journalist as "a lady-like young woman of thirty, with a markedly intellectual countenance, but looking somewhat careworn." It might have been added that she was the daughter of a Dublin practitioner, Dr. Robert Travers, a professor of medical jurisprudence at Trinity College; and that the immediate cause of the action was a letter which Lady Wilde had written him from her summer residence at Bray. This ran :

Tower
Bray
May 6, 1864.

To Dr. Travers:

Sir : You may not be aware of the disreputable conduct of your daughter at Bray, where she consorts with all the low newspaper boys in the place, employing them to disseminate offensive placards in which she makes it appear that she has an intrigue with Sir William Wilde. If she chooses to disgrace herself, that is not my affair; but as her object in insulting me is the hope of extorting money, for which she has several times applied to Sir William Wilde—with threats of more annoyance if not given—I think it right to inform you that no threat or additional insult shall ever extort money for her from our hands. The wages of disgrace she has so basely toiled for and demanded shall never be given to her.

JANE F. WILDE

Although an unpleasant communication for a father to receive, this one ignored it. Miss Travers, however, being less indifferent, held that it reflected on her morals, and instructed a solicitor to bring an action against the writer, assessing the damages to her injured feelings at £2,000.

Lady Wilde entered a defence. This was fourfold : (1) that her letter to Dr. Travers was not libellous; (2) that it was not defamatory; (3) that it was privileged; and (4) that there had been no publication. In fact, she pleaded everything, except that she had not written it.

There were two issues to be settled. One was, had the plaintiff been libelled by the defendant; and the other was, had the defendant's husband been guilty of unprofessional conduct in the circumstances under which Miss Travers was proceeding for redress.

2

The action, which lasted a week, was considered of such importance that it was heard by Chief Justice Monahan and a special jury. Miss Travers was represented by Serjeant Armstrong and Isaac Butt, Q.C.; and Lady Wilde had the services of Serjeant Sullivan* and William Sidney, Q.C.

In his opening address to the jury counsel for the plaintiff whetted the appetites of the audience in the public gallery.

"The particulars I shall have to reveal," he began, "are of so shocking and embarrassing a description that it is my sincere wish that the duty of presenting them had fallen to some other counsel."

"In view of what you tell me," said the Chief Justice, "perhaps, and before you go any further, any ladies who are here would like to leave."

As none of the feminine occupants of the public seats made a move, or evinced any disposition to act on the suggestion, the learned Serjeant, after a pause, shrugged his shoulders, and proceeded with the business before him. Despite the embarrassment he felt, he had no scruples about telling the jury what was alleged to have happened to his client at the hands of Sir William, then Doctor, Wilde. She had, he said, consulted him professionally, but Sir William had conducted himself towards her in a manner that was very far removed from professional; and had "attempted an

---

* Serjeants-at-law occupied a niche between judges and Queen's Counsel, and wore a distinctive dress and had their own Inn of Court. Except in Ireland, they were abolished by the Judicature Act of 1873, and the Society ceased to exist in 1877.

intimacy that should not exist between a physician and a patient."

Oratory was not lacking. The defence quoted the Bible; the prosecution countered with Shakespeare. Serjeant Armstrong's best effort, however, was when he was on the point of putting the plaintiff into the witness-box.

"Gentlemen of the Jury," he began, in a voice that trembled with emotion, "the task of telling you precisely what occurred in Dr. Wilde's consulting-room is beyond me. I must leave the revelation to my unhappy client. All I can bring myself to say about it at this moment has been said by the poet in those memorable words—

> 'She went in a maid,
> But a maid she did not depart!'

When the proper time comes, it will be the sad lot of Miss Travers herself to tell you of the dreadful ordeal to which she was there subjected."

This sounded promising; and the occupants of the public gallery, all agog for further details, pricked up their ears. Before, however, anything more could be said, Serjeant Sullivan sprang to his feet in vigorous protest.

"My Lord," he interrupted, "I really must protest. My learned friend is really going too far. He is bringing a definite charge against a second party, Sir William Wilde. This action, however, is not against him. His presence here is merely as the husband of Lady Wilde. He should, accordingly, be spared unwarranted insinuations."

"I only want the truth to come out," riposted Serjeant Armstrong.

"That is just what I want," was the response, "but

I strongly resent the introduction of slanderous matter."

The observation called for a reproof from the Bench.

"Counsel must really set an example to the younger members of the Bar," said the judge. "There must not be any wrangling. I will not permit it. Such conduct is objectionable."

"As your Lordship pleases," continued Serjeant Armstrong imperturbably. "I have no wish to bolster up my case by indulging in rhetoric or exaggeration. It is quite strong enough without that. I shall now put Miss Travers into the box. There, gentlemen of the jury, she will tell you her sad story. As she does so, you will observe the traces of grief and care on her countenance, resulting from the dreadful ordeal to which she has been subjected. All I can say about it at this stage is that she was robbed of her most cherished possession—her maidenly innocence—by one who, above all, should have remembered the trust imposed in him by virtue of the position in which he stood towards her."

This was the cue for Miss Travers. The feelings of Serjeant Armstrong still being overwrought, he left her examination to his junior, Mr. Butt. In reply to that counsel's questions, she said that she had first consulted Dr. Wilde in 1854, when she was troubled with deafness. Having treated her, he began, she said, "to regard her more as a friend than as a patient". Asked for details, she supplied them promptly enough. He gave her, she said, books to read, as well as theatre tickets, with dresses and bonnets, and "even warm underclothing". He also, she added, wrote her numerous letters, one of which began, "Do come and see me, and I will give you just whatever you want". What Miss Travers wanted was, it appeared, money;

and Dr. Wilde, agreeing, made her loans for various small sums.

All this, if unprofessional, was devoid of anything really objectionable. But, before long, the recipient of these favours did, she said, have something of which to complain.

"What was that?" enquired Counsel. "Was it something serious?"

"Yes, it was. He took me in his arms and begged me to call him William."

"And what did you call him?" demanded his Lordship, as he prepared to take a note.

"I called him a silly old man, and said that he ought to be ashamed of himself."

"When," continued Butt, Q.C., "you refused to call him what he wanted you to call him, what did Sir William tell you to do?"

"He told me to go to the devil, so I went to a solicitor."

This reply appeared to amuse the occupants of the public gallery.

"There is nothing to laugh at," remonstrated Chief Justice Monahan, checking the guffaws. "If any more interruptions occur I will have the Court cleared."

"Tell his Lordship and the jury," went on Counsel, "were you astonished at Sir William's attitude?"

"Yes, I was."

Continuing her story of what, she said, had happened in the surgery, Miss Travers said that, "fearing the worst", she resolved to leave Ireland and visit her brother in Australia. As the passage money, like the cost of an outfit, was an obstacle to achieving her purpose, she put modesty in her pocket and borrowed £40 from Dr. Wilde. But she only got as far as Liverpool, where, exercising her feminine prerogative, she changed her mind about completing the journey and returned to Dublin.

"When you got back," she was asked in cross-examination, "did you have dinner with Sir William?"

"Yes, I did."

"An odd thing to do. What was your reason?"

"Well, it was for the sake of appearances."

"Not very creditable ones," was the dry comment of Serjeant Sullivan.

3

The real interest in the case began when, under pressure from Mr. Butt, Miss Travers told the Court of her experience in Sir William's consulting-room.

"I asked him one day," she said, "to look at a burn on my neck. Suddenly, he put his arms round me, and I fell to the floor and lost consciousness. Dr. Wilde poured water on me, and, as soon as I recovered, he said, 'Pray rouse yourself, or we shall both be ruined'."

"And were you— er—ruined?"

"I was."

"Sensation!" automatically scribbled the occupants of the press-box.

Instead of demanding particulars, Counsel put another question.

"What did you do?"

"I went home in a cab."

It was then that was put the question for which the listeners were all agog:

"You have told us that you were ruined. I do not wish to embarrass you, but does this mean that, during the time you were unconscious, Dr. Wilde attempted to—er—obtain possession of your person?"

"It does. I considered it an outrage, and told him so."

Once more, "Sensation!" was jotted down in the notebooks of the reporters.

A couple of days after the alleged "outrage" Miss Travers received a letter from Dr. Wilde: "Do forgive me. I am miserable and lie in bed thinking of you . . . Be a good girl and don't tell anyone what happened". On Christmas Eve he sent her £20, which she returned. But she returned it by instalments of half a crown and upwards at a time, with occasionally a few postage-stamps.

"I was so upset," volunteered the witness, "that when I next called on him in his consulting-room I drank a pennyworth of laudanum I had brought with me. He made me swallow an emetic and sent me home in a cab."

From this it was obvious that, whatever she was, Miss Travers was no Lucretia, who, according to the classical tale, took such a serious view of a similar experience at the hands of Tarquinius that she killed herself. Instead, however, of following this example, Miss Travers hurried off to a solicitor and invoked the aid of the law.

"Did you have any more letters from Dr. Wilde?" was the next question.

"Yes, I had several. One began, 'I feel for you, but you don't feel for me'; and another said, 'Poor Mary, God help us both. You have nearly killed me. Make your mind easy. Your revenge will be quite successful'."

Miss Travers was certainly bent on "revenge". But she was resolved that it should be on Lady Wilde, by whom she had been "cut", as well as on her husband. Her preliminary step, accordingly, was to publish (with Lady Wilde's pen name Speranza attached to it) a scurrilous pamphlet in which she charged Sir William Wilde with attempting to "take advantage" of her. She sent a copy of it to his wife, who returned it, with a message, "Lady Wilde does not take the least interest in the subject." This attitude rankled. Thereupon, she hired newsboys to hawk the pamphlet in the Dublin streets, and offer it to the audience when Sir William was lecturing to the Young Men's Christian Association at the Metropolitan Hall. Not only this, but she composed some doggerel verses, one of which ran:

> The oculist cured
> I give you my word
> With his own bottle I have dosed him.
> I sent him a drink
> That will cause him to think
> Until his own blushes will roast him!

A copy of this effusion, in which she wrote, "Please hand to her ladyship at dinner", was sent to Merrion Square.

Lady Wilde could stand a good deal. Still, there were limits to her endurance. This being one of them, she wrote Dr. Travers the letter on which his daughter was bringing her action.

4

Giving evidence, Lady Wilde said she had known Miss Travers for several years, and had received her as a dinner guest and allowed her to call. As Miss Travers had afterwards forced her way into the Merrion Square house without an invitation, she had refused her further acquaintance. She had, she added, written to Dr. Travers because his daughter was bringing unfounded charges against both herself and her husband and endeavouring to extort money from them.

"Had you any malice towards Miss Travers?" she was asked.

"Not a bit. My sole object in writing to her father was merely to prevent the pamphlet being pushed into my letter-box, where it could have fallen into the hands of my innocent children. As a matter of fact, my little girl picked up a copy to me and said, 'Oh, mamma, this must be about papa and yourself. What does it all mean, please?' "

Learned counsel had something else to ask.

"In your letter you employed the expression 'intrigue'. Does that imply—er—illicit intercourse?"

"The average reader would not understand it as such."

"Then you also said that Miss Travers 'consorted with low newspaper boys'. What did that mean?"

"It meant that she talked to them, but not for an improper purpose. The boys were only ten years old."

In the course of her further evidence Lady Wilde made one admission that was received with astonishment by all who heard it. In fact, the judge had to ask her to repeat it before he would record it on his notes.

"When Miss Travers," said Serjeant Armstrong, with the air of producing a trump card, "complained to you of your husband's attempt upon her virtue, why did you not answer her letter? What was your reason?"

"Because I was not interested."

"Do you really mean that?" enquired the Serjeant, looking very shocked.

"Yes, I do mean that."

The admission was a tactical error; and, although Serjeant Sullivan attempted to brush it aside as unimportant, the mischief had been done, and the jury were seen shaking their heads and whispering among themselves.

5

Both Serjeant Sullivan and his second string, Sidney, Q.C., put forward a vigorous defence of Lady Wilde. The letter to Dr. Travers, contended the learned Serjeant, was written for the sole purpose of warning him of his daughter's misconduct. But it did not impute unchastity to her. Mr. Sidney, following his leader, declared that Lady Wilde had been "injured, harassed and oppressed to an unpardonable extent by the accusation that her husband had dishonoured her bed". He finished a long speech on a high note:

"Gentlemen of the Jury, the defendant was compelled to write the letter in question to protect herself from a depth of infamy that is without parallel in these courts. This cruel action is launched by the plaintiff to gratify a spirit of revenge and to crush and destroy a once happy home. I cannot believe that you will permit a miscarriage of justice; and I am confident that you will deliver a verdict in accordance with the dictates of your conscience and one which my oppressed, harassed and outraged client demands at your hands."

Butt, Q.C., following Serjeant Armstrong, contested this vigorously. "I am," he declared, in a forensic flight that at times approached rhodomontade, "battling here with the forces of rank and influence arrayed

against me.   The cause I plead is that of a weak and
sadly wronged woman.   Do not dismiss her with a
bleeding heart, dishonoured and disgraced.   Such a
step would be to blot the annals of Irish justice.
Whatever your decision, I will await it at a still
greater tribunal, one where every motive will
become known and the secrets of all hearts be
revealed."

Dropping fustian, learned counsel made a real
point when he directed attention to the fact that
Sir William Wilde had not gone into the box to rebut
the story of Miss Travers.   Then, as a finishing touch
to his speech, he pulled out the *vox humana* stop to its
fullest extent and launched a last thrust at the
defendant:

"When Lady Wilde admitted that 'she took no
interest' in the sad story of the outrage to which
Miss Travers had been subjected, I hung my head in
shame.   Oh, that those terrible words had not been
uttered!   Oh, that I had not heard them!   They
have shocked me and grieved me.   Would that they
could be obliterated from our memory!   Gentlemen of the Jury, you will share my shock and
grief."

"Pray calm yourself," interrupted the judge.

"As your Lordship pleases," returned Counsel,
recovering his composure.

After all this surfeit of oratory, it might have been
thought that there was now nothing left for Chief
Justice Monahan to say on the subject.   None the less,
he had a good deal to say.   His summing-up of the
case took him two hours to deliver.   The respon-
sibility of Sir William Wilde was, he pointed out,
merely that he happened to be the husband of the
defendant; and, although it was undoubtedly libellous,

the letter had not been written or published by him. Nor was there any suggestion that it had been written and sent with his knowledge. Hence, all that concerned the jury was to decide if the letter were true in substance and fact; and, if they found for the plaintiff, to say what damages, if any, should be awarded. "Remember," he warned them in conclusion, "that any such amount will have to be paid by the defendant's husband. If it should please the Almighty to remove him to another world before your decision is implemented, then Miss Travers will have to look to his widow for the recovery of such damages. Lady Wilde should, accordingly, be considered as a single woman."

Thus instructed, and looking somewhat befogged by what they had heard, the jury retired to deliberate among themselves. At the end of half an hour they reappeared in Court.

"Gentlemen of the Jury, have you agreed upon your verdict?" enquired the Clerk of Arraigns.

"Not yet," returned the foreman. "We want to ask a question first."

"What is it, please?" said the Chief Justice, thinking that some knotty point of law which he was prepared to unravel was troubling them.

"Could we have some more coals on the fire in our room?"

"Let it be done," commanded his lordship, signalling to the usher.

Thus assisted to make up their minds, the jury reached a decision within the next ten minutes.

"We find," said the foreman, "that the defendant's letter was not true in substance and fact."

"That," interpreted his Lordship, showing that

nothing was hidden from him, "is a verdict for the plaintiff.   What damages, if any, do you award her?"

"One farthing, and costs against the defendant."

CHAPTER 7

CHANGE OF SCENE

I

A FARTHING damages did not, perhaps, sound worth worrying about. But the verdict carried costs. These were fairly stiff, for, although the cash value of Miss Travers's chastity was assessed by the jury at the equivalent of the smallest coin of the realm, the case had lasted six days, and the fees to counsel and solicitors were not a penny under two thousand pounds. Altogether, that memorable afternoon in his consulting-room must have proved an expensive one to Sir William Wilde.

There was much commiseration expressed for the defendant, but none at all for the plaintiff.

"Of spite, malignity, folly, unwomanly daring and fiendish cunning, it would," wrote Charles Mackay, in the *London Review*, "be difficult to have a more remarkable specimen than that presented by Miss Travers. On her own showing, her conduct does not merit the smallest sympathy."

The *Lancet*, voicing the opinion of the medical profession as a whole, was equally emphatic: "It rarely occurs, where a plaintiff on her own showing admits herself to be indifferent to the obligations of her oath, and in many most important particulars deliberately forswears herself in the witness-box, that counsel adopt her story as completely true, and avail themselves of the opportunity to both outrage and abuse a professional gentleman, knowing that he can have no

possible redress. . . . Sir William Wilde has been
assailed by Miss Travers's counsel in a manner for
which not one word can be urged in extenuation."

"Of Lady Wilde," ran another editorial, "no one
can speak except with sympathy and respect. If
honest indignation and matronly scorn had well
weighed every word, perhaps her communication to
Miss Travers's father would have been more guardedly
—it could not have been more truthfully—expressed.
. . . Few living women have evinced a more chivalrous regard for their personal independence and
honour than this most gifted and justly respected
lady."

But jarring notes were also struck. Thus, Professor
Tyrrell, asked by the ever inquisitive Frank Harris for
his view, said that "the trial simply established what
everyone believed". To this expression of opinion he
added that Sir William Wilde "was a pithecoid
person of extraordinary sensuality and cowardice, and
funking the witness-box left him without a defender".
Nor was he over charitable towards Lady Wilde,
declaring her to be "a high falutin' pretentious
creature whose pride was as extravagant as her
reputation founded on second-rate verse making . .
She gave herself besides all manner of airs".

Although the case was very fully reported and
attracted columns of leading articles, Miss Travers did
not have "a good press" anywhere. As she read
some of the comments on the trial, she must have felt
upset. "Poor wayward woman," was one of them,
"we will not permit you to be your own accuser, for,
if we do so, we must regard you as being very wanton,
rather than excessively silly. We do not, however,
desire to aggravate the bitterness of your self-pro-
claimed degradation."

Miss Travers was so indignant at these and similar comments that a few months later she brought another action.

"She had had the temerity," remarked the *Lancet* (registering shocked remonstrance) "to proceed against our contemporary, the *Saunders' News Letter*, for publishing the opinion of the press with reference to the course she pursued at the former trial. After a full and anxious investigation, the jury found a verdict for the defendant, thus partially endorsing the opinion to which we have already given expression, viz. that from this prosecution Sir William Wilde may safely appeal to the undiminished confidence and respect of his friends. As between the two ladies our sympathies must be with the insulted wife, not with the infuriated spinster."

2

There were plenty of other comments, all of them in a very similar strain. Dublin had not had such a tit-bit of gossip and scandal for years. Of course, some people shook their heads, and, adding sly allusions to "The Wild(e) Knight", whispered, "no smoke without fire". Still, public opinion, as a whole, felt that Miss Travers had drawn on her vivid imagination, and that, in giving her a verdict, the jury had been hoodwinked by the oratory of her counsel.

In connection with this case certain points inevitably suggest themselves. Miss Travers may have had other cards up her sleeve (and probably had some there) ready to be produced if wanted. They were not wanted. But, although her story was uncontradicted, it was also uncorroborated. This, however, was largely due to the attitude of Sir William Wilde's counsel in not letting him go into the witness-box and there give his version of the business. Clearly an error of judgment. In the language of the duello, he had received his opponent's fire without returning it. Chivalrous, perhaps; still, a tactical slip. Nor did he escape scot free. "When," remarked one critic, "an elderly man permits himself to take a paternal interest in a good-looking and intellectual young woman, there is always a danger that he will end by entertaining towards her feelings which are something more than paternal."

As to the letter written by Lady Wilde, this was undoubtedly libellous. What, of course, she should have done would have been to have had an interview with Dr. Travers and asked him to restrain his daughter's questionable activities. But it is always easy to know what to do after the event. For the rest, it may be said that a great deal of very dirty linen had been washed in the worst possible laundry, and that none of the parties to the action had emerged from it with any credit to themselves.

As was, perhaps, only to be expected, the case of Travers *v.* Wilde had an appeal for the Dublin bards. One of them was delivered of a ballad which was chanted at Trinity College smoking-concerts:

> There's an oculist living in Merrion Square
> Who has skill that's unrivalled and talent that's rare;
> And if you will listen, I'll try to reveal
> The matter that caused poor Miss Travers to squeal!

There were several more verses. Unfortunately, the author drew on his imagination for details to such an extent that none of the others are printable.

By the way, Frank Harris (always an unreliable source of information) says that Oscar Wilde, discussing the case with him in after years, declared: "My father got into trouble once in Dublin. My mother stood up in court and bore witness for him. She could not believe that the man she loved could be unworthy; and her conviction was so complete that it communicated itself to the jury, and they brought him in guiltless".

If Oscar, who was a child of ten when the trial was held, really said this, it must be regarded as one of his imaginative efforts. What, however, is far more probable is that Harris, as was his custom, was romancing.

3

In a slip-shod volume of mid-Victorian memoirs, it is said that Sir William Wilde died in August, 1868. If he did, he was, according to the long obituary notices in the Irish papers, not buried until 1876, when he was given a public funeral at the Mt. Jerome cemetery, Dublin. As a matter of fact, the date of his death was April 19, 1876.

The President and officials of the Royal Irish Academy, together with a large body of members, attended the funeral; and, says a report, "as a special mark of honour to the deceased, the mace of the Academy was draped in black". A vote of condolence with the widow was passed at the Academy's next meeting, and, "as a further token of respect to Sir William's memory, the discussion was adjourned".

The medical papers all published tributes to their late colleague. One such appeared in the *Lancet*:

Although it was apparent for some months past that the health of this most eminent member of our profession, and still more famous writer, was failing, the announcement of his death has created a profound sensation throughout Ireland. . . . The obsequies were attended by a vast concourse, including nearly all the leading members of his own profession in Ireland. Those who attended the Boyne excursion of the British Medical Association in 1867 will remember with what erudition, tact and energy he acted as cicerone, an office he had previously filled for the historian Macaulay when preparing his account of the famous battle . . . Sir William Wilde's town house, No. 1 Merrion Square, has for a quarter of a century been the scene of almost weekly reunions of the leading artists and littérateurs of Dublin, and of those foreign countries who happened to visit that city.

Among the many obituary notices was a long one in the *Compendium of Irish Biography*; and another in the *Journal of the Archaeological Society*. Extracts ran:

Sir William Wilde had the happy knack of popularizing and bringing into notice the information entombed in the ancient annals and the drier disquisitions of others. In everything connected with Ireland's history, traditions, literature and relics he was inspired with an impassioned fervour. His love of the antique past was an enthusiasm with him; and all that is strange and beautiful in the ancient art and architecture of Ireland touched him deeply . . . Sir William had unusual gifts and facilities for acquiring knowledge on all subjects on which he wrote, a marvellous memory that no lapse of years seemed to deaden, and a remarkable power of utilizing all he saw and heard. He also had a wide acquaintance with all classes of the community throughout the country; and these were ever ready to give him any information he required.

By the peasantry he was specially loved and trusted, for he had brought back joy and hope to many households. How gratefully they remembered his professional skill, always so generously given, and how, in the remote country districts, he would often cross moor and mountain at the call of some poor sufferer who believed with simple faith that the Doctor would certainly restore the blessed light of heaven to blind-struck eyes.

Among the actions to his credit was one thus recorded by a contemporary:

"When the statue of Thomas Davis, sculptured by George Hogan (originally commissioned at a cost of a thousand pounds, subscribed by his friends and admirers) was refused a site in the City Hall and also in the hall of the Royal Dublin Society it was Sir William Wilde who, as a last resource, suggested its erection over the grave. As this was found to be impracticable, it was erected in front of the former residence of John Keogh. But the weather played havoc with the marble, and Sir William took the necessary steps to have it admitted to the shelter of the mortuary chapel at Mount Jerome, where it now stands."

A circumstance that redounds to the credit of Lady Wilde is that, although they were common knowledge and she was fully aware of them, she ignored her husband's gallantries and liaisons. More than this, when he was dying she uttered no protest to his wish that he should be visited by a woman who was the mother of one of his natural children. Her attitude was not one of indifference, but a genuine desire to let him have this last comfort.

Sir William Wilde had spent three years collecting material for a projected memoir of Gabriel Béranger, a Hugenot by descent and an archaeologist by inclination, who was once a well-known figure in Dublin circles; and on his death Sir William had left a considerable portion still to be written. Regarded by her as a trust, this portion was completed by his widow and published in the *Kilkenny Archaeological Journal*. Some years later it was reprinted as a pamphlet in both Dublin and London, prefaced with a warm, if somewhat florid, tribute to her husband's memory by Lady Wilde:

It is sad to take up the pen fallen from the pale cold hand of the dead, and endeavour, through all the discouraging consciousness of insufficient knowledge, to complete the book left unfinished by a well-trained writer, perfectly learned in all the details of the subject in hand, and whose opinions had weight and authority.

. . . There was probably no man of his generation more versed in our national literature, in all that concerned the land and the people, the arts, architecture, topography, statistics, and even the legends of the country. When engaged on any subject he gathered knowledge from every source, ancient and modern—from history and tradition—and, having sifted all for the truth, he treated the matter exhaustively and left nothing to be supplied or added by any other writer that might follow his footsteps on the same line of ground.

It was the earnest wish of Sir William Wilde that Béranger's sketches, so rich in suggestions for our living artists, and so important to the antiquary and archaelogist, should be published in a volume along with the Journal. He would have undertaken the work himself, even at his own expense, had health and life been spared to him. But it is to be hoped that the project will not fall to the ground; and that the publication of so useful and valuable a book will be accomplished by someone with an intellect as energetic, a mind as well stored with the requisite knowledge, and a heart as zealous for the advancement of Irish art and literature, as were the intellect, the mind, and the heart of Sir William Wilde.

When the memoir was published, Lady Wilde sent a copy, with the following letter, to Edward Clodd, the editor of the *Modern Review*.

1, Ovington Square, S.W.
July 15, 1880.

Dear Sir,

I have the pleasure to forward to you a copy of the last book on which Sir William Wilde was engaged, and hope you will favour me by a notice of it in your *Modern Review*.

I have read your able paper with great interest, in the July number, on the Later Stone Age; and was much gratified to find Sir William's name mentioned with due honour in connection with the crannoges of Ireland, a subject to which he devoted much investigation.

It always gives me the highest pleasure to find that his name and last years are not forgotten by the wise and learned of this age, amongst whom you hold so eminent and distinguished a place.

Believe me to remain,
with much appreciation,
Very truly yours
FRANCESCA SPERANZA WILDE.
(Lady Wilde)

These compliments proved effective; and a glowing notice of the book appeared in the next number of the *Modern Review*.

4

During the course of his long professional career Sir William Wilde had earned a large income from his practice and also from his books and lectures. His estate was valued for probate at approximately £20,000. He left his widow nearly £8000; and his two sons were each left £4000, as was also one of his natural sons, whom he had set up as a doctor and employed as an assistant. The executors, however, when they came to look into matters, found the estate so saddled with debts that the legacies could not be paid in full. As a result, what Lady Wilde received was a pittance of something under £300 a year.

Since this, of course, was not sufficient on which to keep up the Merrion Square house on anything resembling its former standard, she removed from Dublin to London, where her elder son Willie was working as a journalist. The younger one, Oscar, was still an undergraduate at Oxford, having entered at Magdalen in 1874.

As a journalist, Willie had established himself fairly well, and was writing regularly for the *World* and the *Daily Telegraph*. These two organs were an excellent medium for his talent, which, as approved by editors at that period, was inclined to be florid. His pen was a ready one, and he could fill a column without difficulty on practically any subject allotted him. Most of his work was done in the Café Royal, where, with a bottle of brandy within easy reach, he would sit for hours every evening surrounded by a band of

Fleet Street colleagues. When he was asked by an inquisitive companion what he was working at, his customary answer was "at intervals".

As a side line to his journalistic activities, he busied himself with conducting an enterprise which he called the Cigar Club. When (as soon happened) it was wound up for lack of members and insistence on unlimited credit, Speranza was sympathetic. Willie, however, accepted the situation philosophically. "Only to be expected," he said, "of anything that begins and ends in smoke."

But before this happened, he sent out a circular letter to the members:

Dear Sir,

Your attendance is requested at an extraordinary general meeting of the Cigar Club, when the following resolutions will be proposed:

(1) To increase the price of cigars.
(2) To reduce the price of cigars.

Yours faithfully,

WILLIAM CHARLES KINGSBURY WILDE
Chairman

per pro. W. C. K. Wilde
Secretary

When the meeting was held an amendment "That there should be no charge at all for cigars" was ruled "out of order". As a result, the Cigar Club was promptly liquidated.

"You should," said Speranza (who always had a solution for every difficulty except her own) "have got Oscar to address the shareholders."

"Unfortunately, I'm the only one," was the response.

"I liked Willie Wilde," says an intimate.* "He was impulsive, slovenly in person and dress, generous, witty, kind hearted to a fault, unconventional and full of courtesy, a stranger to all pedantry and posing, and a born journalist. Writing came to him quite naturally."

Oscar, for whom he acted as fugleman and sedulously puffed in season and out of season, followed hot on his brother's heels. Describing himself, on coming down from Oxford, as a "Professor of Aesthetics", in 1881 he began his London campaign by publishing (at his own expense) a slim volume of poems.† At the start, however, his tongue proved of more service to him than his pen, and "he talked himself into success", was the opinion of an intimate. Still, he had something beyond mere "talk" in his equipment; and, apart from occasional and modestly requited appearances on the lecture platform, he gradually discovered a more satisfactory niche in the better class magazines and reviews.

Although outshone by his younger brother, Willie Wilde was by no means devoid of accomplishments. He had done well at Trinity College, and, although he did not practise, had been called to the Bar. His good looks, fund of anecdote and amusing tongue made him popular, especially with women. Conspicuous among his feminine admirers was a certain Madame Gabrielli. Apropos, there is a story to the effect that when somebody enquired his reason for wearing a bangle that had once adorned that lady's

---

* *Jimmy Glover: his Book:* James Glover: Methuen.

† *The Athenaeum* dismissed this effort as one which, "when their temporary notoriety is exhausted, will find a place on the shelves of only those who hunt after the curious in literature". When Oscar presented a copy to the Union Library at Oxford, the gift, says Henry Newbolt, was declined by the committee on the ground that "it consisted of plagiarisms from more deservedly reputed poets".

arm, he replied, "I wear it because it's the gift of the Gab". This was an attribute of which he himself had no lack. "In his own way," said a fellow journalist, "he was as brilliant a conversationalist and quite as amusing a companion as his brother." There was, however, no physical resemblance between the brothers. If ever there had been one it was unnoticeable by the fact that Willie grew a beard. "Oscar pays me £250 a year to do so," was how he checked curiosity on the subject.

Between the years 1875 and 1877 the *Dublin University Magazine*,* officially described as "a literary and philosophical journal", printed several poems under the signature Oscar O'F. Wills Wilde. The fact that there was no guerdon other than publication drew a letter of protest from him to the editor. "I hope", he wrote, "that in twelve months the *D.U.M.* may be restored to its true position again, and be able to pay its contributors."

Oscar did not accompany his mother and brother when, in 1880, they first settled in London, but took lodgings for himself in a dingy street just off the Strand. It was after returning from his lecture tour in America that he could afford to remove to the neighbourhood of Berkeley Square. On his marriage, in 1884, he was able, assisted by his wife's modest fortune, to establish himself as a householder at No. 16 Tite Street.

The two ladies, Miss Katherine Bradley and Miss Edith Cooper, who adopted the masculine pseudonym

* "Most of the literary talent towards the middle of the century", wrote W. E. H. Lacky, "was connected with the 'Dublin University Magazine', which had attained a very high place in periodical literature . . . It was imbued throughout with a strongly accentuated Toryism; and although it would be unfair to assert that all its contributors fully shared its politics, there seems little doubt that nearly all were in general sympathy with them."

"Michael Field" for the books on which they collaborated, once accepted an invitation to call there.*

"We visited", they said, "Oscar Wilde, being received by Mrs. Wilde in turquoise blue, white frills and amber stockings. The afternoon goes on in a dull fashion till Oscar enters. He wears a lilac shirt and heliotrope tie. . . . His large presence beams with the *Heiterkeit* of a Greek God that has descended on a fat man of literary habits".

As a general rule, Oscar Wilde did not impress women favourably, at any rate not at a first encounter. Thus, one of them has recorded an unflattering opinion: "Somewhat in awe", she says, "I observed him more closely. He was stout, fair, with a heavy jowl that contrasted strangely with his brilliant eyes which constantly glanced here and there, commanding attention. After dinner he was brought up and introduced to me. Reluctantly I took the pale flabby hand. The aura of his personality repelled me vaguely. He looked like something grown in the dark, like a big pale mushroom".

After meeting Oscar at his mother's *salon* Katherine Tynan also registered dissatisfaction. "My impression of his looks," she records, "was of an immense fat face, somewhat pendulous cheeks, and a shock of dark hair, a little like the Poet Bunthorne."

But it was left for Mrs. Atherton† to express herself still more strongly: "His mouth", she declared, "half covered his face. I declined the prospect of meeting him at his mother's house, and sent a telegram to Lady Wilde, saying that I was in bed with a cold."

---

* *Work and Days from the Journal of Michael Field*, edited by T. and D. C. Sturge Moore: John Murray.

† *Adventures of a Novelist*: Gertrude Atherton: Jonathan Cape.

Mrs. Atherton, however, was notorious for her sharp tongue; and it is conceivable that Oscar had no desire to encounter it.

As a visitor to the drawing-room of Lady Morris, an Irishwoman whom he was cultivating, he also managed to make himself unpopular. "Oscar Wilde", wrote her daughter, "came to our house now and again. My mother could not bear him, especially his mannerism of standing on the hearthrug in front of the fire, with his back to the company; and there he would pose until he got his huge heavy face in the cheval glass above".*

Fortunately for his peace of mind it never occurred to him that he was not everywhere the most welcome of welcome guests. As a general rule, London hostesses were not so particular as Lady Morris, and would consider it a triumph to secure his presence at their houses.

Like his mother, Oscar invited all sorts of people to his parties. A popular comedian, Arthur Roberts, who was once his guest at supper, has recorded† how his host impressed him: "You had", he said, "to be initiated into the mysteries of his conversation before you, as a reasonable person, could understand what he meant. He made a remarkable idol as he sat at the head of the table, with a ridiculous green carnation stuck in his buttonhole".

---

* *An Irishman and his Family:* Maud Wynn: John Murray.
† *Fifty Years of Spoof:* Arthur Roberts: John Lane.

CHAPTER 8

SPERANZA'S SALON

I

THE London of the early 'eighties in which Speranza was to cut something of a figure when, on removing from Dublin, she first settled there, would be unrecognized to-day. A London of which the then characteristic features have now utterly disappeared, never to return. None of the modern amenities. A London without aeroplanes, cinemas, coupons, crooners, gigolos, identity cards, motor cars, taxi cabs, or wireless. The wheels have revolved, but with changes in almost every direction; and matters now considered ancient history then red hot "news". Thus, people still talking of the death of the Prince Imperial in Zululand; trouble in the Transvaal and Afghanistan, and the prospect of more to follow in Egypt; the telephone looked upon as a "toy", and the typewriter as a "Yankee novelty of questionable use"; penny postage to all parts; a budget of eighty millions sterling; an annual expenditure of thirty millions on the armed forces; and an income-tax of threepence in the pound. "Unless we check this mad extravagance," remarked a shocked chronicler, "there is a possibility that some day the tax will be doubled"; and an M.P. was so uneasy that he submitted a resolution, "That this House views with regret the deplorable increase in the national expenditure".

For the rest, changes all along the line. Thus, a London of whiskers and frock coats and bonnets and bustles; statesmen instead of politicians in the Cabinet; "professional beauties" and barouches in the Park; hansoms and growlers in the streets; Irving and Ellen Terry at the Lyceum; Gilbert and Sullivan at the Savoy; melodrama at Drury Lane; tights at the Gaiety; coryphées at the Alhambra; red-nosed "comics" at the music-halls; Pinero and Henry Arthur Jones regarded as promising beginners; Oscar Wilde, Barrie, and Bernard Shaw still awaiting the production of their first plays; pontifical leading articles and verbatim reports of speeches in the newspapers; editors taking themselves seriously; no chit-chat or "social gossip" admitted to their columns; solid and stolid reviews; Leighton and Alma Tadema enthroned at the Royal Academy; acid comments about the Pre-Raphaelites; the works of Tennyson and Browning in Victorian "parlours", and Swinburne interned in a Putney villa; three volume novels from the circulating libraries; yellow backs on the railway bookstalls; Miss Braddon and Rhoda Broughton considered "daring"; Henty and Manville Fenn and Mrs. Henry Wood and Charlotte M. Yonge writing for boys and girls; Meredith and Hardy and Trollope for their elders; and Mrs. Humphry Ward on the point of being brought to bed with the preliminary draft of *Robert Elsmere*.

2

Lady Wilde's first London residence was in Ovington Square. But this was only adopted as a temporary address; and, after a short interval in lodgings there, she moved from the Brompton district to a more fashionable one and took a small house in Park Street, where, ambitious to be acknowledged by the intelligentsia as a modern Madame Récamier, she

set to work to re-establish her Dublin *salon*.* Her
instincts were hospitable, so much so, indeed, that
Arthur Ransome says of them, "She was prepared to
suffer fools gladly for the sake of social adulation".

"At that time" (1884), says a visitor, "Park Street
was as distinguished an address as Park Lane. It
remained so until the contingent of diamond magnates
and gold mining magnates from South Africa en-
trenched themselves in the latter thoroughfare."

By comparison with the spacious ones in which the
Merrion Square receptions had been held, the accom-
modation in the Park Street rooms was extremely
cramped. But to Speranza, who had a fondness for
crowds, it was no matter if her callers were packed into
the drawing-room like sardines in a tin. "The more,
the merrier," she said when greeting them. Acting
on this theory, and assisted by Willie, who shared the
house with her, she sent out cards of invitation to
everybody of whom she could think. She could think
of a considerable number, and the acceptances were
numerous. Some of them came from mediocrities;
others were of loftier calibre. Browning was once
seen among the company, as also was Helen Faucit
(the wife of Sir Theodore Martin). On one memorable occasion Ruskin drove up from Denmark Hill, to
mingle with the gathering. He was not encouraged
to repeat the experiment. What upset him was that
he was accosted by a feminine guest, Mrs. Stannard,
who, although a complete stranger, bore down upon
him.

"I'm Bootles," she said, by way of introduction.
Then, encountering a blank look, she added,

---

* "Lady Wilde used to hold a salon in Belgravia, where in broad daylight
blinds were drawn, shutters closed, candles lit, and she sat enthroned in
artificial splendour to receive her guests": *Letters and Leaders of my Day:*
T. M. Healy.

" 'Bootles Baby', you know. Of course, I'm really John Strange Winter. You know that, don't you?"

Ruskin did not know. Nor did he want to know. Fearful of further disclosures, he fled from the scene and returned to Denmark Hill as fast as his carriage could take him there.

"What an extraordinary woman," he reflected. "I wonder if she is right in her head."

Before he left, however, he renewed an acquaintance, dating from his road-making activities at Oxford, with one of his undergraduate helpers. This was Oscar, described by Peter Quennell* as "a talkative Irish youth who boasted that he had frequently been allowed to trundle Professor Ruskin's private barrow."

"My son has abandoned road-making for verse-making," said his mother.

"For poetry, if you please," protested Oscar.

A second "lion" to be secured was Oliver Wendell Holmes, who had met Oscar during his lecture tour in America. Other visitors from the States were Henry Ward Beecher and Bret Harte, with Mrs. Hodgson Burnett, the author of *Little Lord Fauntleroy* (then much "in demand" at Mudie's) and Gertrude Atherton.

3

"It was considered very intellectual," remarked a visitor from New York, "to frequent Lady Wilde's crushes." This opinion being generally shared, the gatherings became so well patronised that before long instead of one reception two were held each week. A specially warm welcome was always extended to callers from Ireland. One of them, Katherine Tynan,†

---

* *John Ruskin: the Portrait of a Prophet:* Peter Quennell: Collins.
† *Twenty-five Years' Reminiscences:* Katherine Tynan: Smith Elder.

has recorded an account of her first visit to Park Street:

"The few shaded candles at Lady Wilde's afternoon receptions were arranged so as to cast the limelight on the prominent people, leaving the spectators in darkness . . . Presently in came Oscar. He stood in the centre of the room. There was some sort of divan or ottoman there on which Miss Fortescue and he sat for a while in conversation. The shaded lights had been specially arranged to fall upon them." Somebody else who was present on this occasion says, "I met Miss Fortescue, the well-known actress, just fresh from winning her breach of promise case against Lord Garmoyle and getting £10,000 damages, and who was very much the fashion at the moment. Everybody wanted to know her".

An occasional visitor, who must have been rather out of his element in the Park Street *salon* was a red-headed and red-bearded young Irishman. This was Bernard Shaw. "Lady Wilde," he says, "was nice to me in London during the desperate days between my arrival in 1875 and my first earning of an income by my pen in 1885."

But all sorts and conditions would be found attending Speranza's receptions, for she spread a wide net. In one of his books* Oscar afterwards supplied a recognizable picture of a typical gathering:

"It was certainly a wonderful medley of people. Gorgeous peeresses chatted affably to violent Radicals, popular preachers brushed coat tails with eminent sceptics, a perfect bevy of bishops kept following a stout prima-donna from room to room, on the staircase stood several Royal Academicians disguised as artists,

---

* *Lord Arthur Savile's Crime:* Oscar Wilde: Osgood and McIlvaine.

. . . and it was said that at one time the supper-room was absolutely crammed with geniuses."

It is said (but without much foundation) that in a second edition of this book Oscar deleted this passage, since, he felt, "it could be construed as a reflection on his mother's harmless weakness".

Among the company on another occasion was a Miss Potter, a professional reciter, very fond of the sound of her own voice. When enough of it had been heard, Speranza interposed: "My dear, you really must not talk so much. With that impressive face you should always be still—still and grave".

To another young girl who was so "still" that she had nothing to say for herself a different tone was adopted. "My dear, I can see that you have a highly intellectual countenance. We shall hear of you distinguishing yourself in the literary world. I expect great things of you. Do not disappoint me."

That mid-Victorian figure of fun (as Bloomsbury insisted on dubbing him) Martin Tupper, described the Egeria of Park Street as "admirable for both prose and poetry, and her eloquent son Oscar famous for good taste all the world over". He paid a visit to the *salon* shortly after the death of John Brown, a member of Queen Victoria's below stairs entourage whom his royal mistress described as "her personal attendant and faithful friend". In less exalted circles he was described as a "Palace flunkey".

On the death of this paragon, Tennyson was asked to produce an ode commemorating his virtues. When the Laureate declined, on the ground (declared by her Majesty to be "inadequate") that he was not inspired, the Muse of Martin Tupper was more responsive and furnished a threnody. At the request of Speranza he recited it in her drawing-room:

Simple, pious, honest man,
Child of heaven while son of earth.
We would praise, for praise we can
Thy good service, thy great work;
Through long years of prosperous place
In the sunshine of the Crown,
With man's favour and God's grace
Humbly, bravely, worked John Brown.

There was more of it, but his hostess declared that the remainder of this effort should be kept for a second visit.

The critical opinion of Oscar was invited.

"Charming," he said. "I doubt if I could have written portions of it myself. You should arrange to have it set to music by Arthur Sullivan—or, better still, by W. S. Gilbert—and, on the anniversaries of Mr. Brown's death, have it sung very softly by a choir of virgins standing round the Albert Memorial."

4

A woman novelist to receive a warm welcome in Park Street was Marie Corelli, who considered no "literary" gathering to be complete without her presence. Still (and despite what Oscar had called her "Turkey carpet style of writing") as an acknowledged "best seller," perhaps she was not far wrong in her view of her own importance.

It was at a party in South Kensington, described by her as a "grand crush", that Marie Corelli had first met Oscar Wilde. "He kept me," she says,* "no end of a time talking on the stairs. Lady Wilde, his mother, was there in a train-dress of silver grey, with

* *Memoirs of Marie Corelli:* Bertha Vyver.

a hat as large as a small parasol, and long streamers of silver grey tulle all floating about her. She did look eccentric. Mrs. Oscar Wilde,* a very pretty woman, interested me, in a Directoire costume, with a tall Cavalier hat and plume, and a great crutch stick."

Where her own dress was concerned Speranza adopted a style that, while certainly distinctive, was such as to strike observers as odd, not to say bizarre. Thus, it is said that she habitually wore two crinolines under a silk gown that swept the floor, and with it affected an oriental scarf, flounces of lace, a number to rings and brooches, and, as a finishing touch, would crown her head of blue black hair with a gilded laurel wreath.

Like her mother-in-law, Mrs. Oscar also took a special interest in feminine garb. About this date she was persuaded to give a lecture on "Rational Dress for Women", at the Somerville Club. An acid criticism by one of the company declared: "Mrs. Oscar Wilde is utterly devoid of the correct demeanour that should be observed on the platform: she giggles at her own witticisms, and explodes in a titter of laughter when she says something that she thinks especially smart."

Where this matter is concerned, a purveyor of gossip has recorded: "At the conference of the Rational Dress Society in Queen's Gate Hall last week, held under the presidency of Mrs. Oscar Wilde, a letter was read to the gathering from some ladies in America who wished to co-operate in the movement . . . The room was crowded to overflowing, and great interest was exhibited in the subject discussed. No practical result,

---

* "One of the merriest present was Mrs. Oscar Wilde, at that time the pet of London society." *Mayfair News*.

however, was reached by any of the speakers, and the closure was put when the company adjourned for tea."

By the way, another of Mrs. Oscar's interests (and one which she shared with her mother-in-law) was spiritualism. Like many of her friends, she was given to consulting mediums and listening to "raps", and had been taken in by the humbug of Madame Blavatsky.

5

Speranza was personally acquainted with very few of Oscar's friends, either men or women. The list of these included Ellen Terry, Mrs. Langtry, Mrs. Leverson, and Miss Schuster, with Lord Alfred Douglas, Frank Harris, Lionel Johnson, Stuart Merrill, Frank Miles, Robert Ross, Robert Sherard, and Reginald Turner. As no reason was given for not letting her meet any of them except Sherard, she had the sense not to ask for one.

One of them, however, thrust himself upon her. This was that journalistic Barnum, Frank Harris, who was taken to Park Street one day by Willie. Although he was received with courtesy, he afterwards had the impertinence to write of his hostess: "She sat enthroned behind the tea-table, looking like a sort of female Buddha swathed in wraps, a large woman, with a heavy face and prominent nose . . . She 'made-up' like an actress, and naturally preferred gloom to sunlight".

"Lady Wilde," says that sound critic, Coulson Kernahan, "was vanity incarnate—so much 'incarnate' that, in a smallish room, her ample presence seemed to crowd the other women into puny insignificance. Her entry into a room was as if a great ship, with all sails set and bellying in the breeze, had swept into a harbour, scornfully and arrogantly to hustle out of place a few humble fishing smacks."

Bards of even minor calibre were always accorded a warm welcome by Speranza. One such was Robert Sherard,* then at the beginning of his literary career. "Oscar Wilde," he says, "took me to a reception at his mother's house . . . I was presented as having a volume of poems in the press, and was graciously received. Later on, as I was standing talking to Anna Kingsford, Lady Wilde, holding some primroses in her hand, crossed the drawing-room, exclaiming, 'Flowers for the poet! Flowers for the poet!' It was for me they were intended, for she came up and decorated my coat with the posy."

Luther Munday, an individual described by the gossip scribblers as "a man-about-town" (whatever that may be) was a Park Street neighbour; and, since he was supposed to have influence with editors and publishers, was often bidden to the receptions there. Another, but less frequent, guest was W. B. Yeats. "I am going to Lady Wilde's this afternoon," he wrote to Katherine Tynan. "I wonder if I shall find her as delightful as her books." He obviously did have this experience, for, says one of the company on this occasion, "he was greeted as 'My Irish poet'! "

Yeats was much interested in Speranza's studies on the subject of folk-lore, and once invited her to hear him lecture on Sligo fairies at the Southwark Literary Club, with Dr. Todhunter in the chair. "Not being able to come herself," he recorded, "she sent a folk-lore specialist, a big placid clergyman called Ponsonby Lyon."

---

* *Oscar Wilde:* Robert Harborough Sherard: Werner Laurie.

6

The spectacle of Oscar Wilde dutifully handing round the tea cups in his mother's drawing-room did not appeal to everybody present. "He had," says Lady Augusta Fane,* "a fat, clean-shaven pallid face; a head covered with long fair hair, brushed on his forehead and falling on to the collar of his velvet coat; heavy stooping shoulders and enormous white hands, similar to the hands of Epstein's Rima."

The manner in which he struck Brayley Hodgetts, another visitor, was rather different. "I first," he says, "met Oscar Wilde at a dance, to which he came with his bride on his return from their honeymoon. He had completely altered his appearance. His hair was one mass of little ringlets curled tight round his head. He looked, with his thick lips, like a negro painted white."

This was at the period when Oscar was, as a result of a visit to the Louvre, affecting the Nero-like coiffure of the *Vanity Fair* caricature by Pellegrini.

In his account of the scene at the opening of the Grosvenor Gallery Exhibition, which he attended at this date, Charles Hallé says: "Oscar Wilde did us much harm, as he posed as the embodiment of the aesthetic idea; and his repulsive appearance and tedious paradoxes made sensible people weary of the whole thing before they realized what it meant".

Edmund Gosse tells us that Swinburne, who met Oscar at a reception given by Lord Houghton, wrote to a friend in America: "I thought he seemed a harmless young nobody, and had no notion that he

---

* *Chit Chat:* Lady Augusta Fane: Thornton Butterworth.

was the sort of man to play the mountebank as he seems to have been doing . . . I should think you in America must be as tired of his name as we are in London of that of Mr. Barnum and his Jumbo".

But it is only fair to point out that some of those who met him did not endorse these opinions. Thus, "a lady in the midlands," wrote to Robert Sherard, "My mother was simply delighted with his appearance"; and "an Englishman of very high social rank" (grade not specified) declared : "I thought I had never met so wonderful and positively brilliant an individual." Not to be outdone in paying tribute to his friend, Sherard* followed with a gushing description of "that athletic and Apollo-like form, and the singular beauty of features lit up by genius and good nature".

Some of these adverse opinions were not altogether merited, for, although he had put on flesh, Oscar had good features and carried himself well. The average man, however, preferred the athlete to the aesthete and was apt to be a little suspicious of the latter.

Among the women at his mother's receptions to whom his growing distinction did not appeal was Ouida. "Have you," she enquired of Marie Corelli, "read Oscar's 'Prose Poems' in the *Fortnightly*? They are really ludicrously bad. Have you ever noticed what very silly things people of talent can perpetrate? Genius avoids bathos."

True enough, perhaps. Still, Ouida herself was not always above reproach in this direction. Walt Whitman, on the other hand, was complimentary. "Have you met Oscar Wilde?" he wrote to an acquaintance in London. "He is a fine, large

---

* *Oscar Wilde:* Robert Harborough Sherard: Werner Laurie.

handsome youngster, and has had the good sense to take a great fancy to me."

It was at the house of Lady Seton that Elizabeth Robins, then a young actress from New York playing in London, met Oscar Wilde. "I had," she says in her reminiscences,* "appreciation for his conversation, and for the fact that he devoted half an hour to discussing, among other things specially interesting to myself, his impressions of America." In a second passage she follows this up. "I remember," she adds, "that Lady Wilde, his mother, was at that reception— tall, dark-eyed, with a big nose and heavily rouged under a double white gauze veil drawn close like a mask over her features. But she did better than her son. 'You have a dramatic face,' she said, and wanted to know if I had read her book on Norway. Unhappily, I had never heard of it."

"Lady Wilde," says Mrs. Langtry,† who once looked in at the *salon* out of curiosity, "lived a retired life. Sometimes emerging from her seclusion to give an afternoon At-home to the guests invited by her two sons. On these occasions she used to pull down the blinds and light the lamps, even on summer days."

As for Willie, Mrs. Langtry found him "uninteresting". Still, she was impressed by Oscar, and the strange figure he cut among the gathering. "His customary apparel," she records, "consisted of light coloured trousers, a black frock-coat (only the lower button fastened) with a brightly flowered waistcoat blooming underneath, and a white silk cravat held together by an old intaglio amethyst set as a pin." She seems, however, to have forgotten to mention the lily that invariably accompanied this get-up.

* *Both Sides of the Curtain*: Elizabeth Robins: William Heinemann.
† *The Days I Knew*: Lily Langtry.

7

Yet, whatever the uncomplimentary opinions about him held by some of the Park Street habitués, there is no getting over the fact that Oscar was the real "draw" at his mother's receptions. He made himself agreeable to all, and chatted affably to the nonentities there as if he considered them as important as they considered themselves.

Lord Alfred Douglas, in his interesting volume, *Without Apology*, draws attention to Oscar's deep affection for his mother. "He spoke of her always," he says, "with a reverence which was really quite excessive, considering her character and achievements." On several occasions he took his young wife with him when he called in Park Street. Like her mother-in-law, for whom she had a sincere affection, Mrs. Oscar was anxious to be accepted as a literary woman. But, even with her husband's help to smooth the path, this was more than she could accomplish. Still, as a result of his introductions, she did secure a publisher for two small volumes of fairy tales, *Grandmother's Stories*, and *A Long Time Ago*. These, she felt, gave her a footing (if only at the bottom of it) on the ladder which had been mounted by Speranza.

As much as for any other reason, people went to the *salon* to talk. Most of the talk, however, was conducted by Speranza herself, for the company was expected to keep quiet while she delivered her views. "An immense charm," she once told them, "is added to the social circle by the presence of a brilliant, cultured woman, with tact and grace that can encourage our grave and learned men to speak on the subjects they know best. . . . People are growing weary of the flippant grotesque which debases every high thought and fine feeling. It is then that woman's influence and her special graces in refining and raising the tone of conversation are most keenly felt . . . Appreciation is more in the manner than in the words. Sometimes even a single adjective, judiciously selected, is enough. She has but to lift her expressive face to the speaker and murmur—'beautiful'! This one word would conquer the heart of any timid sage or aspiring poet. He is understood at last; and the most seductive of all flatteries to a clever man is the sympathy that listens and comprehends."

But this did not exhaust the subject, for Speranza was always prepared to enlarge on it. "It is," she said to another audience, "especially as a hostess, when she reigns supreme at her own table, that a woman requires most tact, experience, and varied knowledge of life and literature. Then it is her privilege to lead and direct the conversation; with swift tact to turn the course if rocks are ahead—to evade skilfully, encourage sweetly, and repress gravely. And it is only a woman who can touch the curb with so light a hand that she checks without wounding. She allows no freezing ice to form and obstruct the full sail of thought; but by kindliness and grace she stimulates to exertion all the latent mental powers that may be around her. Then everyone looks happy; and good talk flows like wine from a golden chalice. . . . At such times, when all the rich spiritual splendours of intellect are manifested, there is no need of any adventitious aid from other sources of enjoyment. There is talk far above singing; and the soft ripple of Ionian mirth struck from the converse of related souls is a music worthy of a symposium of the gods."

This lecture might have been labelled, "Talking without Tears."

Anything about Lady Wilde was, for journalistic purposes, "copy"; and an American correspondent in London who happened to read these observations sent a note to his New York editor:

"Oscar's mamma, Speranza, has furnished the would-be social folk here with a textbook in an article for a London weekly. She counsels women to beware, in their new freedom of speech, of talking too much. Lady Byron, she says, interrupted her husband while he was at an immortal work, with, 'Am I in the way, Byron?' 'Damnably,' he replied. Speranza adds, 'and Lady Byron deserved it. She ought to have known intuitively that she *was* in the way'."

Speranza should have "verified her references". Had she done so, she would have discovered the same *riposte* attributed (and with more justification) to Carlyle.

8

The Germans gave a useful expression, *schwärmerei*, which can best be rendered as "gush". Such a characteristic was always strongly marked where Speranza was concerned. As a result, she would attach undue importance to quite unimportant things, and herald geese as swans. An amiable weakness, perhaps, and one for which kindness of heart, rather than failure of a critical faculty, was responsible.

This trait found full employment in one of her volumes of essays. Among the subjects dealt with there were "The Bondage of Woman," "Genius and Marriage", and "Suitability of Dress." On the first of these matters she held strong views.

One grows weary of the woeful uniformity of female life and bondage all over the world. Bought or sold for a handful of money at the Equator, or for a bottle of train oil at the Poles, everywhere degraded as slaves, yet expected to have the virtues of saints, and to be the ministering angels of man's life. Fetters and manacles are on all, for law, prejudice and custom have combined to hold a woman in abject bondage for six thousand years.

A sad picture. Still, Lady Wilde could offer a suggestion that would remedy it:

The Queen has already founded an Order for distinguished bravery, and even another Order to reward the faithful service of her household domestics. Would it not then be worthy of her sex and station to institute a Royal Order of Merit for names eminent in literature and art, with title and life income after the ecclesiastical mode— a peerage, in fact, without being hereditary? At present, women assist in supporting every institution of the Empire, yet the Imperial taxes never come back to them in any form of benefit; and they are not even represented in the legislature.

This was written long before the days of feminine suffrage and women M.P.'s at Westminster that have since arisen.

On the subject of "Genius and Marriage", Lady Wilde seems just a little jaundiced:

The musician finds that his wife has no ear for music; the poet's wife generally hates poetry, calls it "stuff", and laments that her husband cannot write paragraphs and acrostics or prize parodies that bring in such quantities of money.

To this she added:

Love gives soul to a woman, but takes it from a man. . . . A man without the influence of love may rise to any height; love is not the absolute require-ment for his development, as it is for woman's. . . . History contains scarcely one instance of a man of genius becoming united to his equal.

After this, her melancholy conclusion was, "Let all genius remain un-wed".

But Speranza had her own solution for the matri-monial troubles of certain geniuses:

Mrs. Carlyle failed to reach happiness because she had ambition without fear, and intellect without a career, and was too self-conscious and proud to be content with a subordinate part in life. She ought to have considered that her existence was really of no importance to the universe . . . Had she married the village schoolmaster she might have been happier.

For that matter, so, too, in all probability would have been Thomas.

9

Owing to the smallness of her income, and her inability to adjust her budget proportionately, London did not do more than meet Lady Wilde's guarded approval.

"Of course, with countless thousands a year," she wrote,* "London is a delightful place. Nothing equals it in the world for splendour and expense, for the magnificence of its houses, horses, and stately dinners. But only about ten thousand persons in

---

* *Notes on Men, Women, and Books;* and *Social Studies.*

London can live this delightful life of love-in-idleness, with all its pleasant varieties and aims. For if one has no thousands a year, nor even hundreds, and creditors become clamorous and tenants get peculiar ideas about rent, the gilt," she considered, "was then very much off the gingerbread."

As a ready means of solving financial problems (but not her own) emigration to Australia was suggested. In order, however, to be fair, the possible drawbacks were admitted:

"At first," she added, "they will probably miss the copious literature of the London press; and life will appear impossible without the solemn *Times*, the genial *Telegraph*, the soothing flatteries of the *Athenaeum*, and the high-toned grace and courtesy of the society journals." Still, on balance, the position would, she felt, be on the credit side, as "even a rest from these things might prove welcome, and bring a tender calm and repose to the overtaxed brain".

Summing-up, her conclusion was: "Out of the five million in Ireland, a million or two of the generation might well be spared for the chances of a nobler life in the New World. The remainder would then have room and land enough to enjoy life at home".

In a long essay on "Irish Leaders and Martyrs" a good deal was said by Speranza about the troubles of her country and the relief from them afforded by the native singers. One passage ran:

During the great outpouring of the spirit in '48, not only the cultured classes, but the toilers and artisans also, seized with the poetic frenzy, wrote and published some verses of singular merit and strong rude power, for Celtic fervour always finds its fullest expression in oratory and song. The

Irish, especially, have natural gifts of copious and fluent speech. They are orators at all times; but under the influence of strong excitement they become poets. In that stormy era, when every nation was reading its Rights by the flames of burning thrones, the Irish poets, mad with the magnificent illusions of youth, flashed their hymns of hope and songs of defiance like a fiery cross over land and lake, over rivers and mountains, throughout Ireland, awakening souls to life that might long have lain dead but for the magic incantation of their words.

After this expression of opinion, it is not remarkable to find the *Athenaeum* critic observing: "Lady Wilde tells the Saxon plainly what she thinks of him, and paints English and Irish characters from the Irish point of view".

This, by the way, was a period when Harold Frederic and George W. Smalley, together with other well-known American journalists, were working in London. Although it was before the age of "columnists", one of their number who had attended the Park Street *salon* cabled a "gossip item" to the *New York Times*, drawing attention to the *Athenaeum* criticism.

The path of authorship is beset with pin pricks. Often from unexpected quarters. A woman novelist, Lady Florence Dixie, thought fit to call one of her heroines Speranza. Lady Wilde did not feel complimented. On the contrary, she registered annoyance.

"It is a liberty," she declared. "Nobody but myself is entitled to this name."

"But the 'Speranza' of that novel is described as the adopted daughter of an earl and marries his eldest

son," said Oscar, endeavouring to administer con-
solation. "Doesn't that make a difference?"

"Not a bit," was the response. "What it suggests
is the *Family Herald* and the servants' hall."

Although he knew that his brother Willie was
preferred to himself, Oscar had the greatest veneration
and affection for his mother. When he was in a
position to do so, he always made a point of assisting
her financially, and seldom called upon her without
leaving a cheque or a banknote behind him. Such
help came in very handy, for in Park Street money was
often "tight"; and stacks of tradesmen's bills and
urgent demands for settlement would litter her desk.

CHAPTER 9

LITERARY FLIGHTS

I

HER own never over large income having shrunk, and being still further cut by the Land League agitation (and the refusal of the tenants of her Irish property to pay their rents) Lady Wilde, on settling down in London, was glad to resume her former literary activities and earn something from their employment. Starting work afresh in April, 1876, she began by contributing a long poem, "The Soul's Questionings", to the *Dublin University Magazine*.*   In the course of this she put a number of problems, but found a satisfactory answer to none of them.   Hence (and making no bones about plagiarizing from FitzGerald) she concluded:

> Earth cannot answer, nor the purple sea,
>   The worlds are silent on the life to be.
>   No human lips have ever told the tale
> Of what may lie beyond Death's sombre veil;
>   Upon that mystery God sets His seal,
>   The Why, the Whence, the Whither, now
>   reveal.
>
> I look on those dark waters of the dead,
>   The wrecks of glorious life are on them spread;
>   Strong branches broken by the storm of night,

---

* An early contributor was Anthony Trollope.   No payment materialising, he called on the editor, "and was told that such articles were generally published to oblige friends and, as such, did not open the editorial cash box. I think I was wronged", was Trollope's protest.   However, he seems to have accepted the ruling, since he allowed another item to appear on similar terms.

133

Fair blossoms blighted are their moon of light.
Yet not a sound is heard along the shore
Save weeping or the Dead that come no more!

In the same number room was also found for another poetic offering which had been submitted by an Oxford undergraduate of Magdalen. To this was attached the signature Oscar O'F. Wills Wilde. It was not one of his best efforts. "We only knew of him," observed a Magdalen contemporary, Lewis Parnell, "as a humorous and objectionable freak who wrote poetry which we rightly judged to be second rate and second hand."

Never without a subject on which to express her views, Lady Wilde drove a busy pen. Apart from her work as Speranza in THE NATION and numerous magazine articles, she was from first to last responsible for a round dozen books, covering biography, history, folk-lore, fiction, and travel. Considered as literature, none of them had any real value, being marked for the most part by a characteristic verbiage and vehemence. Still, they suited their period well enough, and brought her name prominently before the public.

Nowadays the editorial opinion of the fitting receptacle for most of her output would be the nearest waste-paper basket. But Speranza had the good fortune to be writing at a time when it was held a virtue for an author to fill a column when a paragraph would have been ample, and to take up a great deal of space in saying very little. Length, rather than strength, was the approved criterion; and fustian and rhodomontade impressed themselves on the general public, and also on too many of the critics who should have known better. Unless this were the case, it is impossible to account for the fulsome encomiums passed upon much of the output bearing the signature Speranza.

2

A list of Lady Wilde's published volumes is given in the bibliography following chapter 12. Two of these books, *Sidonia the Sorceress*, and *Pictures from the First French Revolution*, were translations from the originals of Meinhold and Lamartine. The second of these attracted the warm approval of Rossetti (whose attention to it had been directed by William Allingham), Ruskin, and Swinburne.

The Sidonia von Bork,* who figures in the study of Sidonia, was Abbess of the Convent of Marienpliess, and an early advocate of what is now called birth-control. This practice, added to witchcraft as a side line, being frowned upon and "regarded with disgust and aversion" by her superiors, led her to be charged with "causing sterility in certain aristocratic families"; and, on being convicted, she was executed at Stettin in August, 1620. After having been lost for years, a verbatim copy of the records of this Pomeranian *cause célèbre* was discovered on the shelves of the Berlin State Library; and it was from this that Lady Wilde prepared her translation. The effort must have been a considerable one, for the volume she produced ran to nearly five hundred quarto pages.†

---

* "Lady Duff-Gordon's brilliant translation of *The Amber Witch* was, with Lady Wilde's translation of *Sidonia the Sorceress*, my favourite romantic reading when a boy." *Some Literary Ladies:* Oscar Wilde.

† In a reference to this volume Sir Edmund Gosse remarks: "How the attention of Speranza was directed to it I am quite unable to report, but it is hardly a paradox to say that this German romance did not begin to exist until an Irishwoman revealed it to a select English circle . . . It obviously retains far more vitality than any other work of this fervid authoress".

Although the translation was well received by competent judges, Lady Wilde's obituarist in the *Dictionary of National Biography* does not appear to have heard of it.

Only one work of fiction is to be found in the output of Speranza. This was a three-volume novel, *The First Temptation*, or *Eritis Sicut Deus*, "a philosophical romance from the German of Marie Schwab".

Since this was a translation, and she had to adhere fairly closely to the original, some odd passages were necessarily reproduced. As an example, two girls are reproved by their spiritual adviser for admitting that they have read Shakespeare.

" 'I am filled with astonishment,' " said the priest. " 'Here I find two young girls initiated into all the mysteries of worldly literature, and who knows what other mysteries which should have remained for years, if not for ever, hidden in their hearts.' "

In a second passage an admonition is delivered by the same authority to a medical student who was "worldly enough" to express admiration for a print of an unclothed Venus.

"Such a shameless picture is calculated to destroy every moral feeling . . . Away with this art worship. It is the most subtle of all poisons because it suits so well the carnal appetite. It is sinful, the lustful idolatry of the age!"

As was to be expected in that Victorian period, Fraulein Schwab's novel, even when its purple passages were toned down by Speranza, had a mixed reception.

"The object of this work," remarked a broad-minded reviewer in the *New Monthly Magazine*, "is to exhibit the pernicious principles of Strauss and Hegel and their followers in their true colours, and to show to what termination they must lead mankind." One would think this desirable enough. Still, in some quarters the book was held to be "daring", because "the model of a great Christian character is markedly lacking".

But everybody did not agree about this; and the considered opinion of the *Hibernian Magazine* was: "This is a tale full of moral significance, a solemn, almost awful, protest against the spirit of scepticism that devastates the age".

As a help to her critics (who might, she felt, otherwise have missed its import) Lady Wilde's *Ancient Legends* volume was prefixed by an explanatory note: "The studies of the Irish past are simply the expression of my love for the beautiful island that gave me my first inspiration, my quickest intellectual impulses, and the strongest and best sympathies with its genius and country possible to a woman's nature".

Lady Wilde's collection of critical studies, *Notes on Men, Women, and Books*, suggested the consumption of such midnight oil and digging into encyclopaedias and works of reference. Thus, a copious stream of historical allusions, elegant extracts from the classics, and choice poetical quotations by the score. If published to-day, indeed, the volume might almost have served for a series of B.B.C. "Talks".

Certain of Speranza's criticisms offered a challenge. Disraeli, Bulwer-Lytton, and Tom Moore were each accorded handsome testimonials; and Philip James Bailey could be declared "one of England's greatest of modern poets". After this there was not much to be said for Tennyson, and nothing at all for Browning and Swinburne. Still, "a psychological beauty, which no imitation has ever reached", was discovered in "The Princess", and, where the "Idylls" were concerned, she made a discovery missed by other critics. This was that they were "full of lines of beauty that send an electric flash quivering through the frame of the reader".

The output of Disraeli and Bulwer-Lytton was very much to Speranza's taste.

> The former, she wrote, has so fully fathomed life that all men seem to him merely as tools and instruments . . . But the glare of his splendid position does not blind him to the darkness gathering on the horizon. In the spirit of Semitic prophecy he sees that we are approaching a great world crisis, and recognizes that the communistic influence is undermining all the thrones of Europe. . . . What is title or ribbon to a man of supreme intellect, who feels and knows how much above all title he stands by right of his intellect? And if he accepted them, it was only to prove to this privileged class, scorned by him in the depths of his soul, that he could be, when he chose, their equal—and their master.

In another passage there was a handsome pat on the back for Bulwer-Lytton:

> It is a relief to turn from the heavily-weighted sentences of George Eliot to the work of a perfectly trained artist in expression like Lord Lytton. But his latest work, 'Kenelm Chillingley', appeals to us with even a stronger feeling than admiration, as the last utterance of one of the most brilliant intellects of the age. It is filled to overflowing with epigram, genial humour and polished sarcasm; profound reflections over life and lofty aspirations towards the highest good, with mocking aphorisms that show the hollowness of modern social life, and satire keen and flashing as the spear of Ithurial when shams and falsehood are to be unmasked. Every thought is philosophy, every word is gold. . . . All the

graces of classical style, the riches of modern culture and the glowing passion which genius alone possesses and radiates are found united in the wonderful golden flow of Lord Lytton's eloquence. The English language is a truly powerful instrument of thought to a practised writer; but no modern writer has swept the range of its chords with so divine a hand as the great dead master, the last echo of whose exquisite music now vibrates through our hearts.

Leigh Hunt was here accorded a panegyric that he had never received from anybody else:

> As a poet, dramatist, essayist and political writer, Leigh Hunt's genius flashed brilliantly and success-fully through all the realms of literature, illuminat-ing everything he touched; uniting grace and melody, power and feeling, wit and good sense, in a degree beyond most of his contemporaries.

The *Athenaeum* did not agree with all these *ex cathedra* pronouncements. "Lady Wilde," remarked its re-viewer, "altogether overrates the late Lord Lytton, and, naturally enough, Thomas Moore. No one, however, with a reputation to lose as a critic would venture to call 'Lalla Rookh' a 'perfect poem'."

3

Some of the women authors to attract the notice of Speranza in this volume fared badly at her hands. Thus, she found George Eliot small beer; and held her *Daniel Deronda* of little account. Nor did she think much of *Middlemarch*, the reading of which "exhausts our patience by page after page of pretentious commonplace, and probably no amount of bribery would induce anyone to read it through a second time. Altogether, *Middlemarch* is a dull work, without any development of that mystic working of a gifted woman's mind foreshadowed in the preface". Still, she was prepared to put in a good word for *Romola*, declaring it to be "a great book to add to literature".

Lady Blessington would appear to have been regarded by this critic as the Marie Corelli of her period. "Why," she enquired, "does she write such twaddle and trash? Novels, tales, reviews, verses, etc., all of the most mediocre nature certainly. . . . There is such a total want of elevation, of feeling, or depth of thought, in all her works that it is impossible to read them with profit, or to remember them with interest."

In the reference to the chatelaine of Gore House there is an item that appears to have been missed by the biographers. This is that she was the first "columnist" on record, and was employed in this capacity by the *Daily News* to furnish (at an honorarium of £400 a year) "exclusive intelligence and gossip gathered from high circles".*

In the work of Harriet Martineau Lady Wilde found "one of the cleverest female intellects of the present age". Still, she held her biographical studies to be "for the most part cruel, scathing, and remorseless . . . Even when she praises, it is with a cold and grudging reticence. In general, she seeks victims for sacrifice, not heroes for worship."

This, as it happened, was well enough observed, for at times Harriet had a vitriolic pen. Thus, she was not above calling Lord Londonderry "a frothy windbag", and Peel a "diplomatic weather-cock".

---

* "She rated her services at double this sum, and threw up the engagement in six months, for which the proprietors of the paper paid her £250." *Illustrious Irishwomen:* E. O. Blackburne.

Palmerston fared little better, and "only inspired confidence by his ability to get out of mischief after he had got into it". Towards her own sex, however, she had honeyed words, declaring, for example, Lady Byron to be "all that is beautiful and good, an angel of mercy, charity and love"; and incense was also burned to the Duchess of Gloucester, and, but in a small degree, to Charlotte Brontë.

In one of her essays Speranza, having strong views on the subject, echoed the "Girl of the Period" diatribe of Mrs. Lynn Linton. Thus, a passage ran:

> The model woman of the 19th century inclines towards a divided skirt, a Newmarket coat and a jockey cap. She carries a cigarette in her mouth, a whip at the end of her parasol, a stiletto in her fan; and in her hand is the roll of resolutions she is to enforce at the next public meeting upon a crowd of men.

Summing up, Lady Wilde reached a sad conclusion with regard to the departed glories of her sex:

> One mourns over the long hair snipped, the flowing train abridged to a bunch or diminished to a bow, the vain and futile endeavour to stimulate what once had noble amplitude and royal significance.

Still, looking ahead, she could see the dawn of better things:

> The woman of the future will never again be the mere idol of a vain worship, the petted toy of a passing hour. . . . As a Queen in the new and wider sphere of intellectual power, she will stand

beside man, his equal and co-worker, giving her aid to the great cause of light and freedom, with all that uplifts human souls from ignorance and degradation.

Like others desirous of literary distinction, Speranza encountered difficulties in securing a market for some of her output. "It is easier," she declared, "to write a book than to find a publisher. This remorseless race stands dragon-like at the portal of Fame's temple; and few, indeed, of the young aspirants survive the combat which is necessary before they enter."

Proud to be regarded as "the Madame Roland of the Irish Girondins," she wrote a long essay on Lamartine's *L'Histoire des Girondins*. In this she gave a readable character sketch of the Egeria of that body:

Her flashing intelligence seemed inspiration. Conscious of the great soul within her, her pride revolted at the homage paid to beings far below her in every endowment, merely because gilded and tinselled with the trappings of society; and the young girl, brought by a servant to see the splendours of Versailles, returned a Republican and the destined instrument for the downfall of monarchy.

4

Lady Wilde's busy pen did not pass unnoticed. In May, 1890, she was, at the instance of Mr. Gladstone,* awarded a Civil List grant of £70 a year, "in recognition of her services to literature." Others to

* One of the signatories to the recommendation on behalf of Lady Wilde was Professor Dowden.

share in the nation's bounty (but to be fobbed off with smaller sums) were Miss Emily Faithfull and a daughter of Dr. Livingstone. Glad as she was to accept such help, in so doing Speranza reflected that she was being treated with less liberality than had been Lady Morgan, an inferior novelist to whom Melbourne had allotted £300 a year.

Speranza held strong views on this subject, and did not hesitate to enlarge on them.

> The actress, the *danseuse*, the singer, she wrote, are all paid lavishly, worshipped and caressed; but the female writers of England work in obscurity, live undecorated, unrecognized, and die without any national tribute to their genius or memory. Italy has made Mrs. Browning's name immortal in the beautiful city of Florence, because of her noble advocacy of Italian Freedom, but England has no memorial to genius. Why should not a statue, or even a bust in Westminster Abbey be decreed to her amongst the gods of intellect? Many of less distinction might be hurled from their marble thrones in the National Valhalla to make room for England's greatest poetess.

It was with reference to this subject that she once published a translation from the German:

THE POET'S DESTINY

The Priest of Beauty, the Anointed One,
Through the world passes the poet on.
All that is noble by his word is crowned,
But on his brow th' Acanthus wreath is bound.
Eternal temples rise beneath his hand
While his own griefs are written in the sand;
He plants the blooming gardens, trails the vine—

But others wear the flowers, drink the wine;
He plunges in the depths of life to seek
Rich joys for other hearts—his own may break.
Like the poor diver beneath the Indian skies,
He flings the pearl upon the shore—and dies!

Discovering, as have other authors, that there is "no money in books", Lady Wilde, anxious to earn some, made a few appearances in the *Pall Mall Gazette*, the *St. James's Magazine*, *Tinsley's Magazine*, the *Lady's Pictorial*, and the *Queen*. None of these contributions had any real distinction or can be said to have risen above the average standard of any alumnus of a "school of journalism".

In marked contrast to her son Oscar (who was always rude to its members and called journalists "those odd-looking people who sell newspapers in the streets") Lady Wilde made a point of cultivating the press assiduously. Reporters in search of "copy" were never sent away empty-handed, but would be plied with enough particulars of her activities to fill a couple of columns.

"In the dimly-lit drawing-room of her ladyship's house," readers were informed by one of them, "the tall stately woman presiding there suggests to visitors the handsome young Irish girl whose rebel Muse once roused to fever pitch the enthusiasm of her native country. Her splendidly patriotic songs and ballads acted as a tocsin call throughout Erin."

After this introductory effort, Lady Wilde was allowed to speak for herself:

"From my earliest childhood I was always passionately fond of books. My favourite study was foreign languages, and I acquired a good knowledge of half a dozen. Politics, too, had a strong appeal. The

Brother Willie consoling brother Oscar on the failure of
his play " Vera "

story of Irish wrongs and sufferings enthralled me. Yet, until I caught the Nationalist spirit, I did not really approve the movement. This was because my family was Protestant and Conservative, and there was no intercourse between its members and those of the Catholic and Nationalist party. It was when I realized that there should be one that I joined the movement."

To another pressman she gave some views that had already done duty in one of her books:

"Ireland is still held in leading-strings by another people; and, after fifteen hundred years of Christian civilization, and seven hundred years of British rule, we are still without commerce, without literature, without a flag, without dignity—in a word, without self-government."

Since this opinion was expressed, the wheel had revolved; and Speranza, returning from the Shades, would now find a very different Ireland.

"You may say," she told a third press-representative, "that just now I am busier than ever with my literary work. I always have a book or two on the stocks. Such leisure as I have left is given up to articles for a number of leading magazines and reviews, as well as for the important one which is being edited by my son Oscar. It is one to which all lovers of literature have been looking forward since its coming was first announced. It is to be called *The Woman's World*, but the exact date when it is to appear is not yet settled. This Jubilee business is disturbing managerial arrangements."

A fourth pressman was granted a longer interview, and made the most of it in a weekly paper:

"Her Ladyship received me with characteristic Irish courtesy. An ardent Nationalist, she spoke with

10

eloquence of the wrongs and troubles of her country. 'The clouds gather,' she said, 'I see no lifting of them, and their dispersal is in a very distant future.'

"I was privileged during my visit to hear the views of Speranza—as Lady Wilde is known in the literary world—on a wide range of subjects. Among these were poetry, legendary lore, and criticism. With regard to this last, she had a definite opinion. 'Criticism,' she declared, 'has become a lost art. Nowadays its practitioners are ignorant and careless. We want another Hazlitt. Nobody among those who followed him has carried on the torch.'

"And what about your own work, with special reference to poetry? I ventured to enquire.

" 'Poetry, as you know,' returned Speranza, 'has always been my passion. In my native country there is still a nest of singing birds. In England, however, poets as a class are regarded with dislike and suspicion. This is wrong. Poets should be endowed by the State. It is obvious that a poet is more important than a Prime Minister. Unfortunately, what is obvious is seldom recognized.'

"Could I be favoured with your ladyship's views on your other fields of activity—journalism and literature?

" 'My son Oscar,' was the response, 'has given an acceptable definition when he said that the difference between them is that journalism is unreadable, and literature is unread. Of course, he was speaking generally, for there are exceptions. Many of them. My first editor, Charles Gavan Duffy, stood out as a meteor. It was in his paper, THE NATION, that I fledged my wings. Poetry and politics were my subjects.'

"Did not your husband, Sir William, also engage in literary work?

" 'He did. In addition to his scientific accomplishments, Sir William's name will always be remembered in connection with his researches in the field of archaeology. Everybody of note sought his acquaintance. When we lived in Dublin my receptions in Merrion Square were attended by men and women of recognized position in the worlds of literature and art. On this account they called me an Irish Madame Récamier. Well, while this was flattering, it was perhaps going a little too far. Still, I did endeavour to have something in the nature of a salon. As you are doubtless aware, I am doing the same thing here, but on a smaller scale, at my house in Park Street.' "

When the interview appeared, its subject distributed a number of copies among editors and publishers.

CHAPTER 10

FRESH FIELDS

I

As a natural result of the uncomplimentary opinions he had repeatedly expressed about those members of the Fourth Estate with whom he came into contact, it is not remarkable that Oscar Wilde himself had to put up with a good deal of adverse criticism from them. He was persistently sneered at and jeered at in *Punch*, caricatured by du Maurier, and lampooned in plays and operas by Burnand and Gilbert, and every music-hall comedian could always raise a guffaw by bellowing, "Oh, don't call me Oscar, it makes me so Wild(e)!"

But, except for his tiffs with Whistler and tilts at the reviewers of his poems, the subject of such attacks received them in good part, and affected to ignore them. He did, however, once enter a protest when he was entered in the visitors' book at a club to which he had been taken by a member as "O. Wilde".

"Pray, who is 'O. Wilde'?" he enquired of the secretary. "There is no such person. I am Mr. Wilde to strangers, and Oscar to my friends."

Although he had been a frequent contributor to its columns, *The World* once paid him a very back-handed compliment in a "social note" which informed readers:

"Postlethwaite may be sneered at and satirised; his ineptitudes may be the joke of smoking-rooms, and the vials of masculine indignation may be emptied over

148

his head. But the hard fact remains that he is in universal request."

When Oscar, naturally enough, registered annoyance, Edmund Yates, the editor, wrote back:

"The article in question was inspired, though not written by me; but I gave distinct instructions that nothing unpleasant to you was to be said in it. I am sorry to find that my instructions were not more closely followed."

Oscar thought they had not been followed at all, and said so.

After a subsequent protest had been made about another allusion to himself, Yates took a firm attitude.

"I have given definite orders that your name shall never again appear in *The World*."

The indignation of Speranza was more pronounced. She had also been much upset when her son's drama *Vera* "failed to attract" in America. A New York criticism, declaring it to be "a foolish, high-peppered story of love, intrigue, and politics, long-drawn-out dramatic rot", caused her to indite a furious response. Oscar, given it to post, had the sense to post it in the waste paper basket.

"Disraeli," said Speranza, when she calmed down, "spoke the truth about critics, since he called them 'the men who have failed in literature and art'."

Disappointed authors had the same opinion.

"I have one instrument I command," Oscar told an interviewer, "and that is the English language."

As commanding-officer, he made his own rules; and, although he proclaimed himself a "Lord of Language", it is doubtful if Lindley Murray and other rigid grammarians would always have agreed with him. Thus, he made no bones about splitting infinitives and adopting the double possessive, and would blandly ignore the convention of not ending a sentence with a preposition.   As an example, in a hint to a would-be contributor, who had offered him an article on "fashionable life in the colonies", he added, "the dress of our colonial ladies should also be treaced of".

Nor would he admit that this could be put better. "Grammar," he said, when challenged by purists, "is all right for journalism, but all wrong for literature"; and the only slips in which he would permit himself to indulge was a habit of confusing "woulds" with "shoulds" and "shalls" with "wills".

2

In the summer o 1887 the financial position of Oscar Wilde was not too flourishing.   Consequently, he was glad to accept the offer of an editorship that a leading firm of publishers, Messrs. Cassell and Co., made him.   This was that of a projected new monthly magazine (or, rather, the revival of an old one) to be called *The Woman's World*.   Although the salary offered was the modest one of six guineas a week— a rate that would nowadays call down the wrath of the Society of Authors and the Institute of Journalists on the heads of the proprietors—Oscar was glad to accept it.   He probably thought it would lead to something better later on; and, as Speranza, whom he consulted, said, "We all have to begin in a small way; and six guineas a week will at least keep you in carnations and cab fares".

Since Oscar Wilde had hitherto had no experience of editing anything (except himself) Fleet Street registered mild surprise at his selection for the editorial chair; and the *Pall Mall Gazette*, always ready to solve a problem, suggested, "Perhaps the idea is to give London a fresh sensation".

But there was nothing sensational in Oscar's editorial policy. Quite the reverse, and, under his direction, *The Woman's World* followed the accepted pattern of similar journals competing for feminine patronage. Thus, there were helpful hints on dress, cooking, furniture, etiquette, with health and beauty culture, and "society gossip". In fact, except for a serial story and "answers to correspondents", nothing was lacking in the make-up. Still, with informative articles on "Early Victorian Bonnets", "Ladies' Colleges at Oxford", and that stock one, "Is Marriage a Failure?" etc., the editorship of *The Woman's World* seemed an odd milieu for a man who had written *Ravenna*.

When he heard of Oscar's prize poem, W. S. Gilbert was not particularly impressed. "It's nothing out of the way," he said to him. "After all, every year at Oxford some young man is bound to win the Newdigate."

One of the editor's first tasks was, with the assistance of Speranza, to assemble a list of contributors. The names of many of them would have been found in the columns of Messrs. Burke and Debrett. Thus, among them were "Carmen Sylvia" (masking the identity of the Queen of Roumania), Princess Christian, the Countess of Portsmouth, Lady Fairly Cuningham, Lady Constance Howard, Lady Dorothy Nevill, and Lady Sandhurst. For the first number he wrote to "Violet Fane" (Lady Currie) suggesting an article on vegetarianism, "which", he said, "in your hands would, I feel sure, make a capital article. Brussels sprouts seem to make people positively blood-thirsty, and those who live on lentils and artichokes are always demanding the gore of the aristocracy." But although it was duly supplied, the contribution did not appear.

Despite his weakness for "titles", everybody admitted to the pages of *The Woman's World* did not wear a coronet; and niches also fell to Mrs. Bancroft, Mrs. Ormiston Chant, Mrs. Jeune, Marie Corelli, Olive Schreiner, and "Ouida". Another to figure on the distaff side of the editorial list was Katherine Tynan. "It is," she wrote, "one of the many kindnesses I owe to Oscar Wilde that he should have remembered me and put me among his contributors."

As the magazine was not an exclusively feminine preserve, articles were also occasionally accepted from men, among them being Oscar (but not Robert) Browning, W. L. Courtney, and Arthur Symons, as well as from the clerical expert* who had written *How to be Happy though Married.*† The honorarium offered contributors was a pound a page. Since, however, the pages were of approximately quarto size, the scale was not quite as liberal as it sounded. Still, even to "see themselves in print" was sufficient guerdon for most of the lady contributors. Certainly, there were no complaints. Indeed, one of their number says of an article she had sent the editor, "I don't suppose he troubled to read it, but the amount of money he paid me for it seemed enormous". A second, and more business-like contributor added to her emolument by selling for £1.10s. the autographed letter commissioning her contribution.

An occasional visitor to the editorial sanctum was Quiller Couch. "I lunched with Oscar Wilde", he

---

* This was the Rev. E. J. Hardy, who had been a master at Portora when Oscar Wilde was a schoolboy there. He afterwards became an army chaplain.

† On its publication this book had been reviewed by Oscar as "the Murray of matrimony and the Baedeker of bliss".

says, "clad in a magnificent astrakan coat". He was, however, not much impressed by what was underneath this garment. "Neither I, nor anybody else," he adds, "considered his work of real value." But this was not quite the case, for Speranza kept a scrap book in which she preserved cuttings of all Oscar's newspaper and magazine contributions. Among these was a poem which has never been reprinted. Just as well, perhaps, for, as its author candidly admitted, it was not one of his best efforts.

3

The newcomer on the bookstalls attracted an early notice in *The Times*. This ran:

The Woman's World, edited by Mr. Oscar Wilde, gracefully got up as it is in every respect, already has taken a high place among the illustrated magazines. Written by women, for women and about women, striking out an original line, it merits the success it has obtained. Mr. Wilde has been fortunate in securing the assistance of many of the best-known lady authors of the day. He has the honour, by the way, of numbering the Princess Christian among his contributors, and she writes with knowledge and sympathy on nursing the sick.

A specially bound copy of the number containing this contribution from Royalty was sent to Windsor Castle; and the letter of thanks acknowledging it was hung up and framed in the office for callers to see and admire.

"A feather in my cap, that," said Oscar with justifiable pride.

According to an editorial pronouncement, *The Woman's World* (the first number of which appeared in November, 1817, more than six months after the editorship had been assumed) was, according to an official pronouncement, to be regarded "as a medium through which women of culture and position could express their views".   For this purpose its controller once made an attempt to secure something from Sarah Bernhardt and suggested several "likely" topics to her.   Sarah, however, was not responsive, and "much too busy" was the manner in which his overtures were met.   As a result, here defeat had to be registered.

Oscar himself supplied a monthly feature, headed "Literary Notes and Book Reviews".   These latter were always full of passages that could be read with pleasure by the authors to whom they referred.   Thus, a translation from the German by a peeress was trumpeted as "most fascinating and delightful", and somebody else's *Gossip with Girls* was declared to furnish "a quite extraordinary amount of useful information on all matters dealing with the mental and physical training of women".   Then there was an encouraging pat on the back for W. B. Yeats, whose early poems were pronounced to be "certainly full of promise"; and of those of Mrs. Craik the verdict was, "This volume chronicles the moods of a sweet and thoughtful nature; and though many things in it may seem old-fashioned, it is still very pleasant to read, and has a faint perfume of withered rose leaves about it".   Henley, however, did not come off so well, for his verses were dismissed as "inspired jottings."

Although (from a desire to extend a helping hand to beginners) he was rather given to over-praise, in his editorial capacity, Oscar could be delivered of a caustic criticism where he thought it required. Thus, of one inferior work of fiction his comment was: "The plot of this novel is the property of Mrs. Henry Wood. We think it should be sent back to her by the next post". Of another book he remarked: "In our opinion only dramatic critics and University Extension lecturers are entitled to misquote the Elizabethans". "Also," says Arthur Ransome, "he railed at 'the shocking bad grammar of Professor Saintsbury'." But his own grammar and syntax were not always impeccable. "Grammar," he said, when challenged, "was made for journalism, not for literature."

In filial fashion, when it was sent him for the purpose, he reviewed his mother's *Ancient Legends**: "The best book since Croker," he declared, "is this volume by Lady Wilde. The humour of it all has given way to pathos and tenderness. We have here the innermost heart of the Celt in the moments he has grown to love through years of persecution, when, cushioning himself about with dreams, and hearing fairy songs in the twilight, he ponders on the soul and on the dead. Here is the Celt, but it is only the Celt dreaming."

No doubt this meant something. Still, it sounds a little involved, and lacking the clarity of Oscar's usual style. At any rate a number of readers seemed to think so. "It means just what it says," they were informed when they put a question to him.

Speranza took an immense interest in everything printed in *The Woman's World*; and, with her characteristic inability to assess values correctly, looked upon

---

* The *Academy* critic did not extend wholehearted support to this view. His considered opinion was, "The writer furnishes no authority whatever for any of the statements she makes, nor any historical account of the legends she has brought together."

the magazine as if it were the *Nineteenth Century* grafted on to the *Quarterly Review*. She herself contributed a poem to the first number, following it with an article, "Irish Peasant Tales", to the second one; and her daughter-in-law, Oscar's wife, wrote on "Children's Dress" and "The History of Muffs". If undistinguished, these offerings were, after they had been touched up (and the syntax and spelling corrected), at any rate competent.

The stories in Lady Wilde's *Irish Peasant Tales* were written simply and with an agreeable departure from the floridness characterizing most of her work. They also contained touches of humour, a quality markedly lacking in her books. The legends, probably culled from what she had gathered in childhood, had an atmosphere, and dealt with fairies, customs, and superstitions. One of these, "St. Patrick and the Witch", relates that, in gratitude for his escape from the unwelcome attentions of a woman sorcerer, the Saint founded a monastery at Lough Dearh. Having completed this work of piety, "he lifted up his hands and invoked a blessing on the shores of Connemara, even a sevenfold blessing. So, ever since the fish are abundant there beyond all places on the coast of Ireland . . . Unhappily, he forgot, before leaving the mountain, to invoke a blessing on the island, so the people of Erin are still pagan in all ways—rakish and prodigal and given to strong drink even to this day— for the blessing of St. Patrick never rested on them, nor on the land or coasts."

Speranza's poetical contribution, "Historic Women", ran to nearly two hundred and fifty lines. Perhaps its length (but not its strength) was due to the fact that, among many others, her list included Cleopatra, Sappho, Jael, Beatrice, Joan of Arc, Charlotte Corday,

Mrs. Browning and Queen Victoria.   After a passing
tribute to each, the poem ended:

Yes, they have lived, these women whose great
    names
        Are graven on the world's history;
Strong splendid souls that chafed at human wrong,
        And Tyranny and servile solitude,
And bonds that strangle nations to the death;
So flung their lives down with a passionate waste
        As incense upon altar sacrifice,
For glory, country, love, or some great cause;
        For a whole people merged in neighbourhood,
Or one, more loved than nations or the world,
        Annihilating even womanhood,
With all its soft tears and compassionate grace,
        When heaven had need of hero hands to strike
For vengeance, people's rights, or liberty,
And who dares judge these women, God-possessed
        With deep prophetic eyes, on whom was laid
                The mission to avenge?

Priestess and victims! through the world's dark ways
Up the great altar stairs that lead to Heaven,
        The torch of Love in her uplifted hand,
        Woman still guides humanity, and best
Fulfils the woman's mission when she tends
The sacred fires of Glory, Faith and Truth
        In human hearts.   True helpmeet for the Men,
When, with a holy, pardoning, saintly zeal
    She draws the erring nature back to God
With bands of love.   Still pleading for the light
In words that weep and tears that speak like
    prayers;
        The guiding Angel of a darkened world
Whose only light can come from Faith and Love!

There was a great deal more of it. Another two hundred lines, in fact, for when she had a subject on which she felt strongly Speranza's pen was apt to run away with her.

4

But despite all the glowing puffs of the editor's friends, after the first few numbers had appeared, the circulation of the magazine went steadily down. Even Harvey, who had discovered the circulation of the blood, could not have discovered a circulation for *The Woman's World*. All sorts of attempts were made to improve it, but they came to nothing. Instead of buying copies, the public kept their shillings in their pockets, or transferred their allegiance to other periodicals. Hence, and as was inevitable, *The Woman's World* was not long for this one.

"We're making a loss, instead of a profit, on each number," was the gloomy announcement of the managing director as he regarded the ever-increasing stack of "returns" cumbering up the office. "How do you account for it, Mr. Wilde?"

"I can't account for it. I am given to understand that the magazine is on the table in practically every West End dentist's reception-room, and that it is read by all the best butlers and leading ladies'-maids."

"Well, what do you suggest to improve matters?"

"I am told by experts that circulation can always be improved by selling more copies. Ever thought of that?"

But this was easier said than done. Accordingly, after giving it a trial for two years, the board decided to cut their losses and bring the magazine to an end.

"I wish you luck in any fresh opening you find, Mr. Wilde," said the head of the firm, "but I'm afraid another salary of six guineas a week is not picked up very easily these days."

"That doesn't worry me," was the airy response. "I have started work on a novel, to be called *The Picture of Dorian Gray*. When it is finished, remind me to send you a presentation copy."

"No money in novels. That's my opinion."

"Still, I think there will be some in this one. Then I also have an idea for a comedy which I shall call *Lady Windermere's Fan*. If it doesn't suit Mr. Dan Leno I shall offer it to Mr. George Alexander for the St. James's Theatre."

"Well, I suppose you know your own business best, but are you really prepared to risk the chance of becoming a successful dramatist?"

"Quite prepared, thank you. Besides this one, I have ideas for a number of other plays. You must come to each of my first nights."

"If there are any, that is."

"Oh, I think there will be several."

Of course, the real reason for the collapse of *The Woman's World* was that Oscar Wilde should not have been appointed to control it. When the novelty of editing, instead of being edited, had worn off he gradually lost interest in the magazine. Office routine also bored him; and he developed a habit of dropping in at irregular hours and not returning after luncheon.

"You always leave very early, Mr. Wilde," once remarked a member of the firm when he saw him putting on his hat and coat twenty minutes after arriving.

"Yes," was the bland response, "but, then, I always arrive very late."*

---

* This was a plagiarism from Charles Lamb. Similarly, when he fancied it, Oscar Wilde was not above helping himself to a remark from one of Scott's novels.

Another point of disagreement with the board was the editor's persistent refusal to attend to business letters. "It's a mistake to do anything else," he said. "I have known a number of young men of talent and promise who, as a result of their absurd habit of answering letters, have soon become complete wrecks."

5

When the guillotine fell on *The Woman's World* its contributors had to turn to and look for fresh channels of employment elsewhere. Lady Wilde soon found one. This was in the columns of the *Pall Mall Gazette*, where, furnished with an introduction to W. T. Stead (whose style was nearly as florid as her own) she contributed critical articles and book reviews. Stead blue-pencilled very little of them. Still, she did once rather impinge upon his good nature. This was when in a burst of confidence he had commissioned her to dissect an anthology of Irish Songs. Instructed to allot it a couple of paragraphs, she wrote enough to fill two columns, in the course of which she took the opportunity to deliver herself of a political essay. One passage ran:

> The utterances of a people, though always vehement, are often incoherent; and it is then that men of education and culture are needed to interpret and formulate the vague longings and ambitions of the passionate hearts around them. . . . Music and song are part of the life of the people; they give a glow to the stormy twilight of their troubled lives, and strength to bear the tragic terrors of a bitter destiny. Nothing really good in a nation's life is ever lost. It remains an influence

Cover of "The Woman's World"

OSCAR WILDE
when editor of " The Woman's World "

for all time; and the people will never go back to the
servile bondage of the soul and spirit that held them
enchained before the fetters were rent and the bonds
broken by the genius and intellectual force, the lofty
teaching and the cadenced words of the men of '48.

For the *Burlington Magazine*, which was officially
described by its editor, Helen Mathers, as "a high
class monthly", she wrote two long articles on "The
Laws of Dress". In one of them she adopted a fresh
pseudonym "Arachne". An extract ran:

> The "Bloomer" costume is admirable for perching
> upon ladders when copying paintings at the
> galleries . . . With regard to the style most suitable
> for the volcanic and revolutionary sisterhood—the
> Communists, Socialists, Women Suffrage speakers,
> Land Leaguers, and others who war against the
> existing order and aim to guide nations it is sufficient
> to indicate that the dress should be short, solid,
> stern, and severe, flat in garniture, skimpy in
> outline, and ready at once for action or flight.

Dress, however, was not the only subject to attract
her pen. There was always something to say about
politics; and the *Burlington* offered a pulpit for her
opinions, which she expressed with considerable
vigour and at length. Apart, too, from these subjects,
Speranza still clung to her first love, poetry.

> It must, she wrote, always form an important
> element in education, because it can be made so
> powerful an auxiliary. It permeates the blood and
> it tinges a nature for ever after. . . . The poetry of
> an age is generally the completest expression of the
> mind of that age, the ultimate and most perfect
> formula to express the height to which thought has

11

reached. It incarnates the highest ideal to which the soul of humanity, viewed in its unity, had sprung. It is not merely the result of the spirit of an age, but the spirit itself. Poetry is, in fact, the enchanted spiritualism of an age.

As is evidenced in her list of published works, Speranza includes *Poems original, and translated from the French, Spanish, Portuguese, Italian, German, Swedish, and Danish Languages.* It would, therefore, be interesting to learn (and she omitted to say) where and when she acquired a knowledge of these tongues. After all, she only went abroad once. This was on a belated honeymoon trip to Scandinavia, with a brief stop in Hamburg and Berlin. Scarcely enough, one would think, to become really fluent.

6

In attempting to arrive at a fair estimate of Speranza's literary worth, one must not ignore her verbose and turgid style, and her undisciplined tendency to over-statement. This sort of thing, however, was very much the fashion at a time when an author was expected to take up a great deal of space in saying very little; and, unless they were given full measure of print, readers were apt to feel that they were not getting value for money.

But the trouble with Lady Wilde was that, where her output was concerned, she wandered (and often floundered) in too many fields. Poetry, philosophy, politics, history, biography, travel, criticism and fiction all engaged her pen. Still, she did know something of, and had a real appreciation for good poetry. If she had stuck to this, she might have produced something that would have helped her to be accepted as a laureate. But she had too many scraps of talent and none of them was properly developed. Still, whatever she lacked in her make-up, it was not an inferiority-complex. "I am," she once asserted, "the acknowledged voice in poetry among all the poets in Ireland." She believed it, too.*

In common with many other writers on political subjects, she would, in order to make her points—as in her famous *Jacta Alea Est* article—put opinions first, and facts second. If, too, she had been fonder of short words than of long ones, and employed fewer adjectives in her descriptive passages, the result would have been better. A sense of humour would also have been helpful. This, however, was denied her.

"I do not compete with the comic papers," she announced, when an editor, wishing to do her a good turn, once asked her to be a little less heavy in her treatment of a subject he had commissioned. Still, one thing is obvious. This is that Speranza could not have earned the good opinion of such sound judges as Sir William Hamilton, Gavan Duffy, Aubrey de Vere, and Stopford Brooke unless at least some of her work had qualities well above the average.

A field which Lady Wilde exploited best was that of the history, legends, traditions and customs of her native land. Of all these she had real knowledge; and, until she let her pen run away with her, she could be trusted to describe them in an interesting fashion. She held the correct view that the proper appreciation of a country's past is best derived from an appreciation of its language, mythology and ancient

* The *Cambridge History of English Literature* has a reference to her output: "Lady Wilde (Speranza) who wrote remarkable rhetorical verses upon the Irish potato famine".

monuments. "The written word," she insisted, "comes last, because it offers the fullest and highest expression of the intellect and culture and scientific progress of a nation." In her *Ancient Legends* she dealt with the "little people", banshees, leprechauns, and poltergeists, in whose activities the more primitive among the peasants still believe, as well as with Ireland's bygone customs, charms, omens and folklore. Because there is a common denominator among the superstitious current in every part of the world, she advanced the theory that, "we are led to believe that there was once a period when the whole human family was of one creed and one language." This theory, however, is not supported by philologists; and even Speranza had to admit that "not more than twenty words which may have belonged to the original tongue have been discovered." But this, she considered, was a failure on the part of the dictionary makers.

In a second folk-lore volume, *Ancient Cures, Charms and Usages of Ireland* she exhibited something like an encyclopaedic knowledge of the subject. Charms for the treatment of almost every imaginable mishap are here given. Many of them, she pointed out, have a religious basis, and consist of reciting an incantation; others (similarly unknown to the pharmacopaeia) depend for their efficiency on the swallowing of mysteriously compounded concoctions distilled from herbs; and philtres and "love potions" for softening hard hearts and winning back the faithless are also procurable.

Some of Lady Wilde's *obiter dicta* in her chapter on "Sketches of the Irish Past" now read a little strangely. Thus: "By a singular fatality no plot laid against Dublin Castle ever succeeded. Once only, during the seven centuries has the green flag waved over it"; and, again: "There is no word so instinctively abhorrent so invincibly opposed to all the prejudices of Dublin society as patriotism. The country of their affections is England". But she could supply the reason, viz. "the inhabitants are a blended race, descended from Danes, Normans and Saxon settlers, and a mongrel Irish". Well, since this opinion was expressed more than fifty years have elapsed.

CHAPTER II

A CHELSEA RÉCAMIER

I

LADY WILDE left the house in Park Street, "owing", she complained, "to the really extraordinary attitude of the landlord in developing commercial instincts and actually wanting to turn the premises into a shop". He also probably wanted his rent which was apt to be in arrears.

Although she could put up with a good deal, Speranza was not prepared to put up with this. The result was that, accompanied by her son Willie, she removed to Chelsea, where she established herself in Oakley Street, a short thoroughfare connecting the King's Road with the Thames Embankment. The number was 146, but this has long been changed. With Carlyle and Rossetti just round the corner, and George Moore not far away in Ebury Street, the "atmosphere", she felt, was as "literary" as could well be expected.

But, after a few months, she lived there by herself, for both her sons had married and could not do more than pay her occasional visits. Of Willie's American bride, Mrs. Frank Leslie, a rich widow, his mother had a high opinion. "With," she remarked, "her many gifts, her brilliant powers of conversation in all the leading tongues of Europe, her splendid residence and immense income, nobly earned and nobly spent, she

may be considered the leader and head of the intellectual circles of New York." But, despite the
possession of these desirable qualities, the union did
not turn out satisfactorily; and before long, it was
dissolved. "It was not Willie's nature to be faithful
even to a rich wife," says Mrs. Jopling, who knew them
both, "and Mrs. Frank Leslie, standing no nonsense,
quickly divorced him."

In one of her essays on the subject, Speranza had a
great deal to say about American women as a class.
Most of it was flattering to them:

> The American woman disdains colourless
> uniformity, and revolts against social usages that
> would limit her bold originality and assertive self-
> manifestation. She is proud, conscious, strong-
> souled, and self-reliant. She is smart, sharp and
> terrible at repartee, and may sometimes be some-
> what fatiguing to an English ear with her voluble
> flow of words. Her gaze is clear and direct; not
> the "stony British stare", but with the large truthful
> eyes of childhood—the eager enquiring glance of a
> candid nature.
> Women in America, whether married or single,
> rule society and do not suffer society to rule them.
> They carry all before them with imperial sway, and
> are the beautiful despots of the land . . . Literary
> women hold a high place in American society, and
> receive more social homage, as a tribute to intellect,
> than is accorded to literary women in Ireland.

2

As in Park Street, so in Chelsea, and Speranza,
anxious to be accepted there as a modern Madame

Récamier, resumed her *salon*. In order not to clash
with the one conducted by Mrs. Ronalds,* who was
"At Home" in Cadogan Square on Sundays, she had
hers on Saturdays. But, by comparison with its
predecessors in Merrion Square and Park Street, the
average Oakley Street gathering was a shoddy one.
No more "lions" could be tempted to prowl there.
Instead of Browning and Ruskin and others of similar
calibre dropping in for a cup of tea and a chat, the
Chelsea gatherings only attracted a crowd of rather
pinchbeck nonentities and hangers-on to the fringes
of the literary and artistic worlds. But, whatever
their claim to recognition, they were made welcome.

These gatherings attracted attention beyond
Chelsea. They were also "copy" for the Peeping-
Toms of the transatlantic newspaper world. One,
the London correspondent of one of them, under the
heading "Society Gossip", furnished his New York
readers with the following account:

> Lady Jane Wilde [*sic*] gives a reception every
> Saturday afternoon to a select assembly of "Intel-
> lectuals" at her Chelsea residence. No refresh-
> ments, other than a cup of tea and a choice cigarette,
> are offered the company, and the drawing-room is
> dimly lit by lanps. A leading figure at her Lady-
> ship's parties is her son, Willie, the elder brother of
> the better-known Oscar. This younger member of
> the family wanders from group to group among the
> guests, chatting affably to all comers, and, when
> asked, obliges the gathering with examples of
> Hibernian wit and sparkling anecdote.

---

* Mrs. Ronalds, in Cadogan Square, secured for her *salon* "lions" of a more
important calibre. One of them was Arthur Sullivan, who accompanied her
at the piano when she favoured the gathering with *The Lost Chord*. Speranza
found Frank Harris a poor substitute.

W. B. Yeats* visited Speranza at the Oakley Street house. "She longed always perhaps," he says, "though certainly amid much self-mockery, for some impossible splendour of character and circumstance. She lived near her son in level Chelsea, but I have heard her say, 'I want to live in some high place, Primrose Hill or Highgate, because I was an eagle in my youth'."

Ever indifferent to public opinion, Speranza had a habit of "speaking her mind", and with results that must at times have struck her hearers as odd. Thus, according to a passage in the reminiscences of Harold Hartley, she once addressed a bashful youth: "When you are as old as I am, young man, you will know that there is only one thing in the world worth living for, and that is sin".

Always something of a stickler for the correct employment of words, she had a stock anecdote which she would retail if she heard anybody make a slip. The story, which was not a new one, was that one day Noah Webster's spouse discovered him caressing a buxom kitchen maid. Registering annoyance, she exclaimed, "I am surprised!" Thereupon Noah, not turning a hair, retorted, "Pardon me, my dear. *You* are astonished. It is *I* who am surprised."

3

Like their predecessors in Merrion Square, the "Saturday At Homes" in Oakley Street were attended by all sorts and conditions. Out of work authors and overworked journalists rubbed shoulders with chartered accountants and chartered libertines;

* *The Trembling of the Veil:* W. B. Yeats: Werner Laurie

demi-reps and divorcées exchanged opinions with musicians and mummers; and a sprinkling of novelists and nonentities, poets and publishers, and reporters and reviewers met in the crowded drawing-room on friendly terms. Lady Wilde was large hearted, and all comers were welcomed so long as they had something to say and kept the conversational ball rolling.

An occasional visitor who, although he had paid tribute to Speranza when she was living in Park Street, must have felt a little out of his element among such a gathering was Martin Tupper. His hostess, however, accorded him a gushing welcome. "We all feel you are quite one of us," she told him.

The reaction of the author of *Proverbial Philosophy* to this assurance is not mentioned by him in his autobiographical volume. If it had been there, it would probably have enshrined an aphorism in all the standard dictionaries of quotations.

A woman visitor, the Comtesse de Brémont, has an odd account of a typical Oakley Street reception which she attended about this period:

"The door at the top of the flight of steps was wide open. No servant being there to announce me, I followed the stream of callers. A difficult task, as the narrow hall was quite packed. . . . I began to grow impatient at the pushing and jostling of the crowd, everyone of whom might have been a celebrity, but celebrities sometimes have sharp elbows and wear heavy boots.

"Finally I reached the door of the reception-room, and stood there, unable to advance or recede. As my eyes gradually became accustomed to the dim light, I could discern faces that stood out with Rembrandtesque effect. In the semi-darkness Lady Wilde loomed up majestically, her headdress, with its long streamers and glittering jewels, giving her a queenly air. She presented several people to me. I managed to retreat into a corner of the room, where I could note its occupants and study the gathering of long-haired poets and short-haired novelists, smartly dressed Press women, and not a few richly gowned ladies of fashion.

"Lady Wilde greeted me with warm words of welcome. . . . I was infinitely moved by the pathetic expression of her large lustrious eyes, and the evidences of womanly coquetry in the arrangement of her hair, and all those little aids to cheat time and retain a fading beauty."

In her book, *Notable Irishwomen*,* a somewhat similar description of a visit to Oakley Street, but at a later period, is given by Miss Catherine Hamilton:

"It was in the winter of 1889 that I first made Lady Wilde's acquaintance. I had an invitation to one of her Saturday 'At Homes'. It was on a dull muggy December afternoon that I reached the house. The hour on the card said 'from five to seven'. When I knocked at the door the bell was broken. The narrow hall was heaped with cloaks, waterproofs, and umbrellas. Anglo-Irish and American-Irish literary people, to say nothing of a sprinkling of brutal Saxons, were crowded together as thickly as sardines. Red shaded lamps were on the mantelpiece, red curtains veiled the doors and windows, and through this darkness I looked vainly for my hostess. Where was Lady Wilde? Then I saw her—a tall woman, slightly bent with rheumatism, fantastically dressed in a long trained silk gown, and from her head floated long tulle streamers mixed with ends of scarlet ribbon.

What glorious dark eyes she had! Even then, and she was over sixty, she was a strikingly handsome woman.

"Though I was a perfect stranger, she made me welcome and introduced me to someone she thought I would like to know. She had the art *de faire un salon*. If anyone was discovered sitting in a corner unnoticed, Lady Wilde was sure to bring up someone to be introduced; and she never failed to speak a few happy words with which to make the stranger feel at home. She generally prefaced her introductions with some such remark as 'Mr. A. who has just written a delightful poem', or 'Mrs. B. who is on the staff of the *Snapdragon*', or, 'Miss C. whose new novel everybody is talking about'."

Robert Sherard has a story which Oscar told him of another celebrity-hunting woman who adopted this curious habit. "She introduced a friend of his as 'Mr. John whose uncle, poor Sir William, had his legs so shamefully mangled on the underground railway the other day'."

In Miss Hamilton's opinion "no more successful hostess than Lady Wilde could be found. . . . What matter that the rooms were small, that the tea was overdrawn, or that there was a large hole in the red curtains? Here was a woman who understood the lost art of entertaining, and made her house a centre of light and leading. Thoroughly sympathetic, she entered into the aspirations of everyone who ever held a pen or touched a paint brush; and, as in Park Street, those who hailed from the Green Isle were always specially welcome".

If at this period she was something of a figure of fun to chance acquaintances and those who met her for the first time, Lady Wilde always inspired her sons with the deepest affection and respect. This was specially noticeable in Oscar, who, whenever he visited her, shed his postures and posings and became very nearly natural. On such occasions, too, he would hand round the tea cups and talk to the nonentities among his mother's guests as if he found their company attractive to him.

4

"Lady Wilde," says W. B. Maxwell,* "lived at Chelsea, in a very small house which she kept darkened with heavy curtains over the windows; and as she, unlike the house, was very large, ungainly too, one wondered how she got about and up and down stairs in the obscurity without an accident. Artificial light was turned on for parties and one saw Lady Wilde as a vast and terrifying person, with a strangely toned voice and a lace-clad head that nodded portentously.

"The company consisted mostly of Irish poets, painters and writers, spoken of as famous by their compatriots, but with names that other people had never heard of until Lady Wilde trotted them out. 'Let me present you,' she would say, 'to Mr. Bryan Maguire, the poet of Killarney.' Other guests were quite vague men and women, friends of the hostess in Dublin, perhaps now visiting London. And there were also a few followers of her late husband's profession, doctors of medicine. Her two sons, Willie and Oscar, were always at the parties, dutifully supporting her. They were unfailingly good sons to her." Mrs. Jopling is similarly emphatic: "Oscar

* *Time Gathered:* W. B. Maxwell: Hutchinson

brought Lady Wilde to see me. I shall never forget
the proud and devoted tone of his voice as he said
'My mother'."

Although compelled at this period to employ some
prose as a medium for earning a livelihood, Willie
Wilde's real ambition was to be accepted as a poet.
During his career at Trinity College he had, encouraged by Speranza, frequently found an opening in
the pages of *Kottabos*, a College magazine edited in
1876 by Robert Yelverton Tyrrell, Fellow of Trinity
College, Dublin. Among his contributions was one
that afterwards suggested a play for his brother Oscar:

SALOMÉ

The sight of me was as devouring flame
Burning their hearts with fire, so wantonly
That night I danced for all his men to see!
Fearless and reckless; for all maiden shame
Strange passion-poisons throbbing overcame
As every eye was rivetted on me,
And every soul was mine, mine utterly—
And thrice each throat cried out aloud my name!

"Ask what thou wilt," black-headed Herod said,
God wot a thing I do crave for prize:
"Give me, I pray thee, presently the head
Of John the Baptist!" 'Twixt my hands it lies.
"Ah, mother! see! the lips, the half-closed eyes—
Dost think he hates me still now he is dead"?

Reviewing this effort, an acid critic remarked:
"Twenty years ago the young man who wrote as well
as this was an exception. Nowadays, the exception
is the young man who, if he writes at all, does not
write better."

"Your sonnets follow all the accepted rules," was the verdict of Oscar. "Anyway, they each have fourteen lines, with two rhymes in the octave and two in the sextet. All the same, Willie, you had better stick to prose."

Notwithstanding his brother's criticism, Willie Wilde was a cut above a mere poetaster. One of his contributions to *Kottabos* would, if unsigned, have been taken for one by his brother:

FAUSTINE

Because bright jewels my fair bosom deck,
And Love's hot lips close press'd, cling fast to mine,
Because rose-garlands crown the cups of wine,
And all Love's ministers are at my beck,
Think you I mourn—repent—or ought I reck
How tongues wag? Think you I weep and pine,
Shedding salt tears as bitter salt sea-brine,
Because his arms lie warm around my neck?

Look you, we live but once—this life I know;
No other wot I of beyond the tomb—
I laugh to scorn your devils down below—
Your torture-fires—your everlasting gloom!
I seek no heaven, I dream no God above,
I fear no hell, save living without love!

This last line was an echo of Adrienne Lecouvreur's plaint, "*Que faire au monde sans aimer*".

Many years afterwards Ouida,* then in Italy, wrote to a friend in England:

"I knew Oscar Wilde very well. He sent me *Dorian Gray*, and I *did* understand it. I do not think he is a clever man. He was a successful poseur and

---

* *Ouida:* Elizabeth Lee: Fisher Unwin

plagiarist. He was essentially the *cabotin*. 'I have written three comedies in one year,' he said to a friend of mine, and my friend replied, 'A great exercise of memory!' The Italian papers assign him a much higher place than that which he held in London society. I am most grieved for his mother, a talented and devoted woman who has had nothing but sorrow all her life."

Mrs. Asquith* (as she then was) also recorded her impressions:

"The first time I ever saw Oscar Wilde was in May, 1888, at a garden-party given by Lady Archibald Campbell. . . . I observed a large, flat, floppy man in unusual clothes sitting under a fir tree surrounded by admirers. . . . To me he appeared like something monstrous and unreal thrown into a world of human beings ready to applaud, but not to accept any of his views upon life."

5

In view of the smallness of her Civil List pension, and the refusal of the authorities to increase it, Speranza felt that she was not getting a square deal from the country of her adoption. "The State," she wrote, "surely ought to consider the importance of preserving genius from low cares; and Parliament might pass a Bill to exempt the race of the gifted from taxation. For these brilliant beings are necessary to the world. They supply the life, the phosphorus, the divine fire, the grace, beauty, and charm of existence; and the nation in return should relieve them from all the mean burdens of prosaic and parochial claims."

This suggestion, no doubt, touched responsive chords in the breasts of other authors experiencing the *res angusta domi*. But, perhaps because they did not

---

* *More Memories:* Margot Asquith: Cassell and Co.

SPERANZA
as Madame Récamier in Chelsea

Sketch by HARRY FURNISS

OSCAR WILDE
" Apostle of Culture "

happen to be geniuses themselves, it fell on deaf ears where the Chelsea municipal authorities were concerned, and demand notes for rates and taxes continued to be delivered at 146, Oakley Street. Hence Speranza's sad reflection: "Life has become a mean and ignoble scramble for the mere means of living; and all sensitive natures behold with dismay and terror the vile servitude of the intellect to the baser needs of life, and the degradation of the noblest instincts of the soul which the strife for money entails".

About this time, possibly smarting from some of the reviews of her own books, she contributed a long article, "Endymion, a Study", to the *Burlington Magazine*. In this she suggested that all literary criticisms should be withheld until an interval of three weeks had elapsed from the date of the publication of the books concerned.

Now, she wrote, an unhappy author is given but a few days to live, and, after a week or so, the best work, it may be, of a man's life falls into oblivion; the excitement is over, the interest dead, and the critics set to work again with their exhaustive reviews upon some other theme—the nature of elephants, perhaps, or monkeys, or the "intelligent turnip"— and the name of "Endymion" is heard no more.

It is not often that a Prime Minister writes a novel, especially one in which he is supposed to introduce all his friends and acquaintances, while professing to deal with celebrities of the past. So the critics, one and all, fell upon Lord Beaconsfield's latest work, ere it was yet a day old, with a terrible and fierce voracity; tore it limb from limb in extracts and summaries, and scattered the *disjecta membra* far and wide over the broad pages of the dailies and weeklies. Yet, why this eager haste? Why should it be necessary for all the critics to rush at once upon a book, tear the heart and life out of it, and then fling it dead upon the shelf, to be named or thought of no more?

Although comprehensive as it was, her gamut did not include the art of playwright.* None the less, Speranza took an interest in the drama and often visited the theatre. "A twelve-months' training," she wrote, "should, at a dramatic college, be considered indispensable to every girl's education." Her favourite actor was Charles Kean, whose "Richard III" she found "a glorious triumph of art and genius. All that the most consummate artist or poet could conceive as necessary to the delineation of this wonderful creation of Shakespeare he realised. . . . Kean's very silence at times thrilled one with a sense of coming horror that no words could awaken".

As to the fashion in which the playwright should acquit himself of his task, Speranza had her own ideas. "The language of the drama," she said in an essay on Calderon, "everywhere should be that in which the highest passion and excitement of a nation finds natural utterance; and as iambic verse when blank approaches nearest to lofty English prose, therefore it is the most thrilling in the highest drama— for the drama is meant to represent, not a visionary world, but intense phases of actual life."

Enlarging on this subject, she added in another passage:

All civilization is going the same path, for the whole science of happiness now is to forget; and at

---

* In 1887 a "Speranza Dramatic Society" was formed by a body of enthusiasts in a London suburb. It was short lived; and although she was fond of advertisement, there is no record that Lady Wilde gave it her patronage.

the theatre alone can weary humanity hope to find "the waters of forgetfulness". Life is becoming such a tangled mass of claims and duties, such a feverish flush of evanescent excitement, such a desolating flood of small observances that kill all great thoughts, such a poisonous growth of weeds that choke the good seed till no soil is left for a serious purpose or a deep passion to take root in, that we all long to fling off the whole burden at times; to forget the weary treadmill of social customs and usages; to end the vain strivings between desires high as heaven and the iron limitations of a cruel fate strong as the gates of hell; and peace comes to us best at the theatre. Therefore, the weary, overworked, exhausted slaves of society throng the theatres everywhere seeking rest without dullness and excitement without effort.

An admirer of her talent, she wrote to Geneviève Ward: "Mr. Forbes Robertson was here yesterday. He is very charming and has an enthusiastic opinion of your genius. Mr. W. G. Wills was also here, and spoke much of you. You have awakened me to a new life".

"Poor old lady!" says Miss Ward in her reminiscences. "She was beginning to need awakening very much at that time. She had fallen into the sere and yellow leaf, not only of mere old age, but of a sense of misgiving as to the future, and it was her hard fate to live to know the worst."

"To the bitter end," says Boris Brazol (on the questionable authority of the Comtesse de Brémont) "she believed in the innocence of her son. Hers was a pathetic sorrow into which the sympathy of the most devoted friends dared not intrude."

CHAPTER 12

SPERANZA, THE LAST PHASE

I

As the years advanced, Speranza refused to acknowledge that, with them her day might have passed. "A woman," she held, "should never voluntarily resign her place as a social power. She may lose the attractions of youth, but the fascination and charm of manner and conversation will remain." Yet, none the less, something must have troubled her, for, with the passage of years, she made desperate attempts to conceal their inevitable toll. Accordingly, where her personal appearance was concerned, art was summoned to assist Nature. Although lipsticks had not then been invented, powder and rouge and the posticheur's skill were available for overcoming ravages and effecting necessary running repairs. As a further help, she continued to make a practice of shutting out daylight as much as possible, and kept her drawing-room in almost total obscurity. Pathetic, perhaps; still, not unfeminine.

"Lady Wilde, when I knew her," says W. B. Yeats,* in his *Four Years*, "received her friends with blinds drawn and shutters closed that none might see her withered face, and longed always perhaps, though certainly amid much self-mockery, for some impossible splendour of character and circumstance."

In one of his *Letters to the New Island*, for September, 1889 (published by the Harvard University Press), Yeats has an entry:

---

* *Four Years:* W. B. Yeats: Werner Laurie

"Lady Wilde still keeps up, in spite of London's emptiness, her Saturday afternoon receptions, though the handful of callers contrasts mournfully with the roomful of clever people one meets there in the season. There is no better time, however, to hear her talk than now, when she is unburdened by weary guests, and London has few better talkers. When one listens to her and remembers that Sir William Wilde was in his day a famous *raconteur*, one finds it in no way wonderful that Oscar Wilde should be the most finished talker of our time."

Although they did not always stick to her, Lady Wilde always stuck to her old friends. One of their number for whom she had a special affection was an American woman, Anna, Comtesse de Brémont, who, on returning to England from a trip abroad, received a letter asking her to call:

> 146 Oakley Street,
> Chelsea,
> January 30, 1890.

Dear Comtesse,

My sincere congratulations on your safe arrival from all the perils of South Africa.

I hope you have brought home a dusky King, bound to your chariot wheels as victim!

I am at home as usual on Saturdays, and will be happy to see you if you care. Miss Otis, the N.Y. journalist, will be here; and I want to hear all about your new book that is announced in the paper.

I am very busy just now, with numerous claims on my time and thoughts, so I can only see friends on the one day.

> A vous toujours,
> FRANCESCA, LADY WILDE.

In response to this invitation, its recipient betook herself to Oakley Street. "I found Lady Wilde at home", she recorded, "but the Saturday receptions seemed to have lost some of their popularity. There was no crowd, only a few faithful habitués.

"When the first enthusiasm of her greeting had subsided, I was conscious of a subtle change in the atmosphere of the dim old room; something was lacking. There was no longer the joyous spirit of intellectual *camaraderie* that had made the dingy surroundings bright with the interchange of wit. Lady Wilde no longer shone forth in her wonderful brilliant manner. A cloud seemed to have fallen on the house. It appeared to be no longer the Mecca of literary aspirants.

"I was infinitely moved," adds the Comtesse, "by the pathetic expression of her large, lustrous eyes, and the evidences of womanly coquetry in the arrangement of her hair and all those little aids to cheat time and retain a fading beauty. She posed in that dim dingy room like the *Grande Dame* she was by right of intellect."

A curious account of one Chelsea gathering which, accompanied by Miss Corkran, she attended, has in her *Adventures of a Novelist*, been recorded by a second visitor from America, Gertrude Atherton:

"Lady Wilde lived in a tiny house in an obscure street. The gas was presumably cut off, for the hall was pitch dark, and the drawing-room—some eight feet square—into which the miserable slavey conducted us, was lit by three tallow candles. But the strange figure that rose as we entered received us with the grand air. She might have been a queen graciously giving a private audience. . . . The room was close and stuffy, the furniture as antiquated as herself. She talked in a weak quavering voice, mainly of the triumphs of her exalted son, although she soon drifted back to the past, when she had been one of the lights of Dublin with her literary and political *salon*, the words of wisdom that flowed from her facile brain to an admiring world over her romantic *nom de guerre*. But to present circumstances she made no allusion; and the walls seemed to expand until the dingy parlour became a great *salon* crowded with courtiers, and the rotting fabric of her rag-bag covering turned by a fairy's wand into cloth of shimmering gold in the light of a thousand wax candles."

2

All this was true enough, perhaps. Still, Mrs. Atherton had a habit of giving odd, not to say cattish descriptions of the people she met. Thus, she found George Moore, "looking like a codfish wooed by a satyr". How Mrs. Atherton struck George Moore is not recorded.

Mrs. Atherton's* visit had occurred at a period when her hostess was suffering a series of bitter blows and hard knocks. Poverty had come in at the Oakley Street door, and was stopping there. All that Speranza had with which to keep the wolf away was her Civil List grant of £70 a year. Too proud to accept help from her friends, she was often hard pressed, with the result that expeditions to the pawn-shop were not unknown. "Poor thing," says Mrs. Atherton, "she always remains in my mind as a leaning tower of courage." Still, whatever she

* *Adventures of a Novelist:* Gertrude Atherton: Jonathan Cape

lacked at this period, it was not a roof over her head. "The rent was paid me by cheque from Mr. Oscar Wilde," wrote her landlady, Mrs. Albert Broom.

A point that does not seem to have struck anyone was that there was—for those who knew where to look for it—something of a parallel between the careers of Jane Francesca, Lady Wilde, and that other, but earlier, flashing Dublin figure, Sydney, Lady Morgan. Thus, the husband of each was a doctor and knighted; each conducted a "salon"; and each endeavoured to secure a foothold in the literary world. Then, the initial effort of Lady Morgan was also a collection of poems, followed by volumes dealing with the history and traditions of Ireland; and, ever an ardent champion of the oppressed, she plunged into politics and discussed vexed questions with a vigour that sounded a fresh note in contemporary journalism. But "Glorvina" (the *nom de guerre* of Lady Morgan) had better luck than had Speranza. Her vogue continued longer; poor in quality as they were, she amassed a round sum of £20,000 from her books; and, above all, she was spared the unmerited buffets and hard knocks that befell Lady Wilde's last years.

But if they enjoyed considerable popularity, "Glorvina's" books did not enjoy a "good press". The leading critics poked fun at them and looked upon her output as fair game for ribald and adverse comment. "If," wrote the *Quarterly Review* of one of her novels, "we were in Lady Morgan's confidence, we should advise the immediate purchase of a spelling book, of which she stands in need"; and another of her works was declared to be "characterized by bad taste, bombast and nonsense, general ignorance, falsehood, licentiousness and impiety". Still, as a set off to this, she could quote the *Athenaeum*: "So long as wit, fascination, and beauty of style have power over the soul, and so long as goodness, gaiety and dashing spirits are in the ascendant, so long may we expect a public for the works of this writer".

Lady Morgan, in her diary has, under the date of 30th October, 1826, an entry: "A ballad singer was this morning singing underneath my window in a voice most unmusical and melancholy. My own name caught my ear, and I sent Thomas out to buy the song. Here is a stanza:—

> " 'Och, Dublin city there's no doubtin'
> Bates every city upon the sea.
> 'Tis there you'll hear O'Connell spoutin'
> An' Lady Morgan making tay.
> For 'tis the capital of the finest nation,
> Wid charmin' pisantry on a fruitful sod
> Fightin' like divils for conciliation,
> An' hating each other for the love of God!' "

Once, when pressed for the wherewithal to meet some troublesome bill, Speranza invited a dealer, Walter Spencer,* to inspect her bookshelves and make a bid for any volume he wanted.

"Lady Wilde," says Mr. Spencer, "received me in state, that is, she welcomed me from a dais at the far end of the room, like a queen on a throne. 'Look around, Mr. Spencer,' she said regally, 'and tell me what you wish to buy.' "

Having picked out a few volumes, the visitor enquired the price at which she would sell them. She answered with splendid indifference "Whatever you wish to offer".

---

* *Forty Years in my Bookshop:* Walter Spencer: Edited by Thomas Moult: Constable.

The offer was £10. "She seemed pleased and accepted it readily, saying I might call on her once a fortnight at eleven o'clock in the morning as long as I felt there was a parcel worth giving £10 for."

3

These last years of Lady Wilde were saddened by ill-health, poverty and increasing loneliness. The Oakley Street drawing-room was now deserted by its former habitués; and the receptions that once drew crowds to her *salon* there, with people angling for invitations, had to be abandoned, since nobody beyond a few nonentities took the trouble to attend them. Speranza's star in the literary firmament had set. It had now become an ancient light. The once tempestuous flood of material she had poured out was checked; she wrote with ever-increasing difficulty; and when it was written, she had ever-increasing difficulty in finding a market for what she offered. Nobody wanted her poetry; editors returned her essays; and publishers stopped asking her for books.

It was at this juncture that, having read but not fully understood, something of Swedenborg, she turned to spiritualism for comfort, and endeavoured to "get into touch" with that mysterious but uncharted region which its adherents vaguely describe as "the Beyond". But although the hired mediums who conducted séances for her in Oakley Street produced full measure of "raps", and caused tables and chairs to revolve and furniture to jump round the room in the dark, the "messages" they interpreted were disappointing. Still, their recipient swallowed them far enough to begin a book on the subject. Half way through, however, she dropped it and busied herself with something else that promised better results. As it happened, many years earlier, she had projected a similar work; and to this end she had translated a couple of volumes for a series called *The Spiritual Library* which were issued by a Belfast firm. A third volume, *God and the Spiritual World*, was planned to follow, but other activities intervened and the idea was abandoned.

Always prepared to try anything once, and having heard of a woman medium who was declared to be *en rapport* with the departed, she was persuaded by a friend to attend a séance.

As soon as the lights had been extinguished and a "sympathetic atmosphere" created, the medium announced, "There is a spirit here. He is an elderly man with a long white beard, who says his name is William. He wants to speak to you. Please listen carefully and do not ask him any questions."

The announcement was followed by a barrage of raps on the walls and a series of gasps and moans from the medium. When they died down, a cockney voice made itself heard.

"I am with you, dear. I am very happy, and hope you are very happy, too, also our little boys. As you have artistic tastes, you should try to write a book. That's all, so I must go now."

Asked her opinion of this experience, Speranza was not complimentary. "I thought it all rubbish," she said. "If William was really speaking to me he would have known that my two sons are not 'little boys', but are grown men of forty. He would also have known that I've written a dozen books."

"You haven't got faith," said the friend who had introduced her to the medium.

"No, but I have got common sense," was the

response. "That medium woman was a humbug. Anyway, she was not up to her work, or she'd have found out something about me beforehand."

The same disappointing experience awaited Speranza when she consulted a succession of astrologists, palmists, and clairvoyants peering through glasses darkly. For all their glib assurances and boasts of being "in touch" with the past as well as with the future, none of them was of any real service. She would have done better to have saved her money. Of this she had little to spare.

"Spiritualism doesn't help," was her sorrowful reflection. "Nothing helps me now."

In the darkened room where she sat brooding hour after hour and day after day, all she had left with which to occupy herself were memories, the memories of seventy years. Alone with her thoughts, dim spectres came out of the past to confront her. Pale ghosts that would not be dismissed. An odd sequence of them.

As she looked back across the years, a long succession of half-forgotten memories—some faded, others clear and distinct—was unrolled. She saw herself a bright eager girl discussing politics with her father's friends and planning a new order for Ireland; Gavan Duffy's encouragement, and her poems and essays in his paper; the famous *Jacta Alea Est* contribution and the stir for which it had been responsible; trips to Punchestown; strolls under the burgeoning trees in the Phoenix Park with a brilliant young doctor for a companion; the coming of romance; marriage and children; the Merrion Square receptions to the intelligentsia of Dublin; the accolade bestowed on her husband; attendance at the Castle Drawing-rooms and State balls; the unpleasantness of the Travers *v.* Wilde business and its aftermath; her husband's death; widowhood and removal to London; the *salon* she established there; and what she regarded as literary triumphs to follow. Now, all gone, and as if they had never been. In their place now nothing but bitter disappointment and devastating shocks. No comfort from her children. One son, Willie, as good as dead, for he had long ceased to come near her; the name of the other no longer to be even whispered. Now nothing to look forward to but increasing financial anxiety, ill-health, old age and loneliness. A disheartening prospect.

With perhaps a premonition of what was inevitably to follow, she set down her last fleeting thoughts in verse:

DEATH WISHES

Oh! might I pass as the evening ray
Melts in the deepening twilight away;
Calmly and gently thus would I die,
Untainted by ills of mortality.

Oh! might I pass as the silver star
That glitters in radiant light afar.
Thus silent and sorrowless fade from sight,
Lost in the deep blue ether of night.

Oh! might I pass as Aeolian notes,
When over the chords the soft wind floats;
But ere the silver strings are at rest,
Find an echo within the Creator's breast.

It was not quite in this fashion that the end did come. Ever gallant, she made pathetic attempts to rise superior to the buffets that continued to be showered upon her. The struggle, however, could

not be prolonged indefinitely. Run down in health,
during the spring of 1896 she caught a chill. Refusing
to give in, for some days she battled against its
advances. But it had been neglected too long.
Complications followed. On a morning in February
the struggle ended; and her landlady, entering her
room, found Speranza dead.

"Acute bronchitis," was the entry on the medical
certificate. But for the look of the thing, the diagnosis
might well have been "inanition."

Three days later, on the afternoon of February 6,
a solitary hearse, escorted by a couple of undertaker's
men in seedy garments, bore the coffin from the
Oakley Street lodging house to its place of sepulture
in Kensal Green cemetery. A simple funeral, unmarked by the presence of mutes or wreaths or any of
the Victorian trappings of woe that the custom of the
period considered appropriate and their lack as
indicative of disrespect. Of all those who had known
the dead woman when she was a figure to command
interest and attention, only a little handful of mourners
gathered round the grave to pay a last tribute to the
memory of Speranza.

An "In Memoriam" card, prepared by her son
Willie, read: "Jane Francesca Agnes Speranza, Lady
Wilde, widow of Sir William Wilde, M.D., Surgeon
Oculist to the Queen in Ireland, Knight of the Order
of the North Star of Sweden".

There was something odd about this description.
The dead woman was certainly not christened
"Speranza" since this was merely a pen name adopted
for her literary work. Nor is there any authority for
"Agnes". Prior to her marriage, she always signed
letters by her maiden name, Jane Francesca
Elgee.

A somewhat florid inscription, said to have been cut on her tombstone, is given in what purports to be an account of the funeral. As it happens, however, there is now no inscription; nor is there any tombstone or other memorial in Square 127, the spot where she was buried. This is because, since Lady Wilde's relatives did not meet the charges for a permanent sepulture, after the lapse of seven years her remains were transferred to a common and unmarked grave. All things considered, the omission is far from creditable to the family.

Kensal Green Cemetery, the last resting-place of Speranza lies in the Paddington district and is one of the largest in London. First opened in 1832, the necropolis contains an abundance of memorials in the shape of monumental urns, broken columns, medallions and tablets, together with other funeral trappings erected by surviving relatives in pious memory of the departed. Among those to be buried there are the Duke of Sussex and his sister the Princess Sophia, Michael William Balfe, Charles Kemble, William Mulready, Tom Hood, Leigh Hunt, Thackeray and Anthony Trollope; and in the Roman Catholic portion is the vault of Cardinal Wiseman. Thus, royalty, art, literature, music, church and stage are all represented. Nor are the lesser callings omitted, for a circus proprietor, a ballerina, a pill-manufacturer, and the widow of the Reform Club cook have also found their last resting place in the Kensal Green necropolis.

4

Although there was nothing small or petty in her character, the obituaries, taken as a whole, were not

altogether charitable to the memory of Speranza. As
so often happens, her eccentricities of dress, her little
vanities and conceits, her unsupported claim to be
accepted as a literary genius of the first water, her
posturings and posings, and her pathetic attempts to
establish a *salon* and to be regarded as a modern
Madame Récamier were remembered and made fun
of; but her generous impulses, high courage under a
long succession of unmerited rebuffs, and the bitter
sorrows that clouded her last years were forgotten, or,
for the most part, ignored.

Still, this was not the case everywhere; and among
the few obituary notices, written with knowledge and
sympathy, was one that appeared in the columns of
the *Athenaeum*:

"The announcement of Lady Wilde's death suddenly reminded many of us that she had only now
ended her sorrows; and it could not but revive many
memories of old days in Dublin when she was the
centre of much intellectual society, when 'Lady
Wilde's Saturdays' were the most characteristic *salon*
in that city, when her eccentricities excited little
comment, and her talents commanded much appreciation. . . . Unfortunately, she professed to value
intellectual culture not only above all else, but as the
only object in life; and this grave mistake brought
upon her tragic consequences. Yet those who can
testify from intimate knowledge of her sentiments, and
who had reason to probe her inmost feelings when the
strain of society was not upon her, know well that
under the mask of brilliant display and bohemian
recklessness lay a deep and loyal soul and a kindly
and sympathetic nature. . . . Bereaved of her husband, and assailed by misfortunes for which the only
sympathy was silence, she finally hid herself in the

SPERANZA—in old age

greatest of all hiding-places, London; and fled the light of day, bearing her heavy cross in silence and stoical patience under the cover of darkness and the cloak of oblivion. None of her old friends can regret that her sufferings are now ended."

The literary editor of a morning journal also contributed a descriptive sketch that was on the whole well balanced:

"A curious and picturesque figure, once prominent among us, has just passed from the social life of London and Dublin. This was that of Speranza, Lady Wilde. A very brilliant woman in her earlier days, she retained her vivid powers as a conversationalist to the end. On the death of her husband, she left Dublin and settled in London. There she soon became well known to a large circle and at her house in Chelsea she presided over a sort of *salon* where one met a number of people connected with the world of literature and art. As long as she had health and strength, Speranza took an active interest in everything that concerned the intellectual welfare of her native country, Ireland. Not unnaturally, perhaps, she was the subject of many an anecdote, some of which were doubtless apocryphal. But while one might occasionally smile at her eccentricities of manner and dress, it is unquestionable that everybody who knew her best had a high opinion of her, and a very real admiration for her culture, her courage, her eloquence, and her sincerity."

"The note of her character," began a paragraph in the *World*, "was loftiness. She did not perceive small things; her soul was as high as her imagination was fervent; her enthusiasm was fresh; and her heart was tender and true." The *Freeman's Journal* also paid a tribute: "A woman of the most versatile attainments,

genuine intellectual power and commanding character".

But perhaps the best and fairest summing-up of the
career of Jane Francesca, Lady Wilde, was that of a
woman (Miss Corkran) who had once written of her
in rather different terms:

"If her talk was often foolish, and even repre-
hensible, her own life was honourable and courageous
and never mean. Though she liked interchange of
thought, she never gossiped or listened to scandal.
She was fond of solitude, and realized the joy that
comes not from outer things, but from the depths of
the inner being. Her talk was like fireworks—
brilliant, whimsical, flashy. She was most incon-
sistent, and in many ways foolish. But in great
adversity she was brave, indeed heroic, and went
through terrible ordeals; and though she felt the
pinch of poverty, she was always ready to help those
who were worse off than herself."

Possibly there was a modicum of reason for some of
the disparaging criticisms that had been expressed by
people who really knew little of her. After all, and
as A. J. A. Symons has pointed out, "To say nothing
but good of the dead is a pious convention which has
reduced biography to the level of memorial sculp-
ture".

Where Speranza was concerned, "obituary"
would have been here more applicable than
"biography".

There is little more to be added to the chronicle of
this Madame Récamier of Dublin and London.
Always a woman of impulse, she ever allowed her
heart to rule her head. If, during her seventy years,
she did many a foolish thing, and some that were
regrettable, she never did a mean one. Hence, when

the final balance is struck, and the debits and credits adjusted, it will be found that the balance on the whole is in favour of Speranza, Lady Wilde.

It is not of all of us that this can be said.

BOOKS BY SPERANZA, LADY WILDE

JACTA ALEA EST

An exact transcript from the copy in the National Library of Ireland.

THE Irish Nation has at length decided. England has done us one good service at least. Her recent acts have taken away the last miserable pretext for passive submission. She has justified us before the world, and ennobled the timid, humble supplication of a degraded, insulted people, into the proud demand for independence by a resolved, prepared, and fearless Nation.

Now, indeed, were the men of Ireland *cowards* if this moment for retribution, combat, and victory, were to pass by unemployed. It finds them slaves, but it would leave them infamous.

Oh! for a hundred thousand muskets glittering brightly in the light of heaven, and the monumental barricades stretching across each of our noble streets, made desolate by England—circling round that doomed Castle, made infamous by England, where the foreign tyrant has held his council of treason and iniquity against our people and our country for seven hundred years.

Courage rises with danger, and heroism with resolve. Does not our breath come freer, each heart beat quicker in these rare and grand moments of human life, when all doubt, and wavering, and weakness are cast to the winds, and the soul rises majestic over each petty obstacle, each low, selfish consideration, and, flinging off the fetters of prejudice, bigotry, and egotism, bounds forward into the higher, diviner life of heroism and patriotism, defiant as a conqueror, devoted as a martyr, omnipotent as a Deity!

We appeal to the whole Irish Nation—is there any man amongst us who wishes to take one further step on the base path of sufferance and slavery? Is there one man that thinks that Ireland has not been sufficiently insulted, that Ireland has not been sufficiently degraded in her honour and her rights, to justify her now in fiercely turning upon her oppressor? No! a man so infamous cannot tread the earth; or, if he does, the voice of the coward is stifled in the clear, wild, ringing shout that leaps from hill to hill, that echoes from sea to sea, that peals from the lips of an uprisen Nation—'We must be free!'

In the name then of your trampled, insulted, degraded country; in the name of all heroic virtues, of all that makes life illustrious or death divine; in the name of your starved, your exiled, your *dead*; by your martyrs in prison cells and felon chains; in the name of GOD and man; by the listening earth and the watching heaven, I call on you to make this aspiration of your souls a *deed*. Even as you read these weak words of a heart that yet palpitates with an enthusiasm as heroic as your own, and your breast heaves and your eyes grow dim with tears as the memory of Ireland's wrongs rushes upon your soul—even now lift up your right hand to heaven and swear—swear by your undying soul, by your hopes of immortality, never to lay down your arms, never to cease hostilities, till you regenerate and save this fallen land.

Gather round the standard of your chiefs. Who dares to say he will not follow, when O'BRIEN leads? Or who amongst you is so abject that he will grovel in the squalid misery of his hut, or be content to be

flung from the ditch side into the living tomb of the
poorhouse, rather than charge proudly like brave
men and free men, with that glorious young MEAGHER
at their head, upon the hired mercenaries of their
enemies? One bold, one decisive move. One instant to take breath, and then a rising; a rush, a charge
from north, south, east and west upon the English
garrison, and *the land is ours*. Do your eyes flash, do
your hearts throb at the prospect of having a *country*?
For you have had no country. You have never felt
the pride, the dignity, the majesty of independence.
You could never lift up your head to heaven and glory
in the name of Irishman, for all Europe read the
brand of *slave* upon your brow.

Oh! that my words could burn like molten metal
through your veins, and light up this ancient heroic
daring which would make each man of you a LEONIDAS
—each battlefield a Marathon—each pass a Thermo-
pylae. Courage! need I preach to Irishmen of
courage? Is it so hard a thing then to die? Alas!
do we not all die daily of broken hearts and shattered
hopes, and tortures of mind and body that make life
a weariness, and of weariness worse even than the
tortures; for life is one long, slow agony of death.

No! it cannot be death you fear; for you have
braved the plague in the exile ship of the Atlantic,
and plague in the exile's home beyond it; and famine
and ruin, and a slave's life, and a dog's death; and
hundreds, thousands, a *million of* you have perished
thus. Courage! You will not now belie those old
traditions of humanity that tell of this divine God-gift
within us. I have read of a Roman wife who stabbed
herself before her husband's eyes to teach him how to
die. These million deaths teach us as grand a lesson.
To die for Ireland! Yes; have we not sworn it in a

thousand passionate words by our poets and orators
—in the grave resolves of councils, leagues and
confederations. Now is the moment to test whether
you value most freedom or life. Now is the moment
to strike, and by striking save, and the day after the
victory it will be time enough to count your dead.

But we do not provoke this war. History will
write of us—that Ireland endured wrongs un-
exampled by any despotism—sufferings unequalled by
any people—her life-blood drained by a vampire host
of foreign masters and officials—her honour insulted
by a paid army of spies—her cries of despair stifled by
the armed hand of legalized ruffianism—that her
peasants starved while they reaped the corn for their
foreign lords, because no man gave them bread—that
her pallid artisans pined and wasted, because no man
gave them work—that her men of genius, the noblest
and purest of her sons, were dragged to a felon's cell,
lest the people might hear the voice of *truth*, and that
in this horrible atrophy of all mental and physical
powers, this stagnation of all existences, whoever
dared to rise and demand wherefore it was that
Ireland, made so beautiful by God, was made the
plague spot of the universe by man—he was branded
as a *felon*—imprisoned, robbed, tortured, chained,
exiled, murdered. Thus history will write of us.
And she will also write, that Ireland did not start from
this horrid trance of suffering and despair until
30,000 swords were at her heart, and even then she did
not rise for vengeance, only *prepared to resist*. No—
we are not the aggressors—we do not provoke this
terrible war—Even with six million hearts to aid us,
and with all the chances of success in our favour we
still offer terms to England. If she capitulates even
now at the eleventh hour, and grants the moderate,

the just demands of Ireland, our arms shall not be raised to sever the golden link that unites the two nations. And the chances of success *are* all with us. There is a God-like strength in a just cause—a desperate energy in men who are fighting in their own land for the possession of that land. A glowing enthusiasm that scorns all danger when from success they can look onward to a future of unutterable glory and happiness for their country. Opposed to us are only a hired soldiery, and a paid police, who mere trained machines even as they are, yet must shudder (for they are men) at the horrible task of butchery, under the blasphemed name of duty to which England summons them. Brothers many of them are of this people they are called upon to murder—sons of the same soil—fellow-countrymen of those who are heroically, struggling to elevate their common country. Surely whatever humanity is left in them will shrink from being made the sad instruments of despotism and tyranny—they will blush to receive the purchase-money of England which hires them for the accursed and fratricidal work. Would a Sicilian have been found in the ranks of Naples? Would a Milanese have been detected in the fierce hordes of Austria? No; for the Sicilians prize honour, and the stately Milanese would strike the arm to the earth that would dare to offer them Austrian gold in payment for the blood of their own countrymen. And heaven forbid that in *Ireland* could be found a band of armed fratricides to fight against their own land for the flag of a foreign tyrant.

But if, indeed, interest or coercion should tempt them into so horrible and unnatural a position, pity, a thousand times pity for those brave officers who vaunt themselves on their honour. Pity for that brave soldiery whose Irish valour has made England illustrious, that they must stain honour, and fame, and profession, and their brave swords, by lending them to so infamous a cause. Ah! we need not tremble for a nation filled with a pure and holy enthusiasm, and fighting for all that human nature holds dear; but the masters of those hired mercenaries may well tremble for their cause, for the consciousness of eternal infamy will unnerve every arm that is raised to uphold it.

If the government, then, do not come forward with honest, honourable and liberal concessions, let the war active and passive commence. *They* confide in the discipline of their troops—*we* in the righteousness of our cause. But not even a burning enthusiasm—which they have not—added to their discipline, could make a garrison of 30,000 men hold their ground against six millions. And one thing is certain—that if the people do not choose to fight the garrison, they may *starve* them. Adopt the Milan method—let no man sell to them. This passive warfare may be carried on in every village in Ireland, while more active hostilities are proceeding through all the large towns and cities. But, to gain possession of the capital should be the grand object of all efforts. Let every line converge to this point. The Castle is the key-stone of English power; take it, destroy it, burn it —at any hazard become masters of it, and on the same ground from whence proceeded all those acts of insult and infamy which aroused the just retribution of a people's vengeance, establish a government in whom the people of all classes can place confidence.

On this pedestal of fallen tyranny and corruption raise a structure of nobleness that will at once give security and prestige of time-honoured and trusted names to our revolution. For a people who rise to overthrow a despotism will establish no modification of it in its place. If they fight it is for absolute independence; and as the first step in a revolution should be to prevent the possibility of anarchy, the men elected to form this government ought at once to take the entire progress and organization of the revolution under their protection and authority. It will be their duty to watch that no crime be suffered to stain the pure flag of Irish liberty. We must show to the world that we are fitted to govern ourselves; that we are, indeed, worthy to be a free nation, that the words union, liberty, country, have as sacred a meaning in our hearts and actions as they are holy on our lips; that patriotism means not merely the wild irresistible force that crushed tyranny, but reconstruction, regeneration, heroism, sacrifice, sublimity; that we have not alone to break the fetters of Ireland, but to raise her to a glorious elevation—defend her, liberate her, ennoble her, sanctify her.*

Nothing is wanting now to complete our regeneration, to ensure our success, but to cast out those vices which have disgraced our name among the nations. There are terrible traditions shadowing the word *Liberty* in Ireland. Let it be our task, men of this generation—descendants of martyrs, and sufferers, and heroes, to make it a glad evangel of happiness— a reign of truth over fictions and symbols—of intellect over prejudice and conventionalism—of humanity over tyranny and oppression. Irishmen! this resurrection into a new life depends on you; for we have all lain dead. Hate, distrust, oppression, disunion,

---

* This sounded suspiciously like an echo of Sydney Smith: "The moment the very name of Ireland is mentioned, the English seem to bid adieu to common feeling, common prudence, and common sense."

selfishness, bigotry—these things are Death. We must crush all vices—annihilate all evil passions—trample on them, as a triumphant Christ with his foot upon the serpent, and then the proud hallelujah of Freedom will rise to heaven from the lips of a pure, a virtuous, a regenerated, a God-blessed people; and this fair land of ours, which now affrights the world with its misery, will be one grand temple, in which we shall all kneel as brothers—one holy, peaceful, loving fraternity—sons of one common country—children of one God—heirs together of those blessings purchased by our blood—a heritage of freedom, justice, independence, prosperity and glory!

THE AMERICAN IRISH

This excessively rare pamphlet by Lady Wilde is not in the British Museum. A copy of it is in the Library of Congress at Washington.

THE record of Irish wrong is an old story now, scarcely remembered by the nation whose struggles for conquest so long made Ireland a land of mourning and woe. But the tale still lives in Irish hearts with enduring vitality. Every century has witnessed some fierce effort to throw off the foreign yoke, and every generation adds new names to the long roll of martyrs and victims doomed to suffer for the vain but beautiful dream of national independence. Exile, confiscation, the prison and the scaffold form the leading chapters of Irish history, even to our own day,—an endless martyrology written in tears and blood.

Yet, some good has come of the evil.

Many holy and sacred things spring up in a nation's soul from the seed sown by persecution. Suffering purifies and refines, and a people learns the value of coherence and unity mainly through oppression. There is also something ennobling in the love of an object out of self, in the devotion to an abstraction called Country; in this dream of freedom, with all the word means, dignity, honour, sufferings; many fine-toned chords in the nature of her people, a gentle courtesy of manner that is almost reverential, and a power of winning sympathy and love which the stolid English organization, with its plethoric prosperity and self-centred egotism, is entirely without.

It is remarkable also that wherever the Irish are

located in other lands, they never forget the old country. It is still the Mecca to which their eyes are ever turned. Exile even seems to intensify their feelings, and the fearless oratory of passion glows with a fervour that would be impossible in the police-ruled country at home. In America, more especially, free speech knows no limit with regard to the past and future of Ireland. Irish festivals are celebrated here with words that clang like swords, while memorial rituals keep the martyrs of freedom for ever living before the eyes of the people. Armed clubs are named after the chief leaders of Irish revolt, and solemn processions mark the anniversary of each national tragedy, for there are no triumphs to record in Irish history. The Greeks of old wrote the names of their heroes in letters of gold upon the walls of their temples; the Irish must search for the names of their heroes on the walls of a prison.

This consecration of revolt, this canonization of the victims of rebellion has a powerful influence on the self-reverence, and self-respect. It will be a sad day, perhaps, for the higher national life when Ireland has no more dreams, and the country no more martyrs, for then an ideal will have passed out of the life of the people, and a nation without an ideal aim on which to concentrate the passions, soon becomes hopelessly materialized, inarticulate, and dull. The subtle, spiritual fancies and the finer issues of human feeling are stifled by the sensuous, selfish enjoyment of the actual and the present, and nations, as well as individuals, become hard and cold without the divine impulse of sacrifice and self-abnegation. To the impassioned nationality of the Irish, with its large indefiniteness of aim and instincts of resistance, may be also due much of the fervour of Irish eloquence.

All oppressed nations are eloquent. When laws forbid a people to arm, they can only speak or sing. Words become their weapons, and the Irish armoury is always bright and burning. Nationality, this dream of an ideal future, illumines their poetry and oratory, their music and song with a vague splendour of passion and pathos, and preserves even the common speech and popular literature of the people from the coarseness and vulgarity so obtrusively characteristic of the English lower classes.

Ireland, then, has some compensation for her young generation of American Irish. It kindles a bitter and deathless indignation in their hearts, and, like a warm gulf stream, the tide of their passion surges across the Atlantic to raise the temperature at home to the revolutionary heat, which, in these days, generally culminates in the endeavour to found a Republic. It is singular that the Irish may live for years in England, yet they never acquire the English manner —calm, grave, and self-possessed; nor the English habits of order and routine; nor even the English accent,—while in America they rapidy become Americanized, bold in speech, audacious in enterprise, self-asserting in manner, and, above all, republican in sentiment. No Irishman returns from America loyal to monarchy. On the contrary, he laughs to scorn the old bonds of servile feudalism, with all its superstitions of class worship; and his opinions soon gain many followers. The American flag holds the place of honour at all popular demonstrations in Ireland, and is always greeted with enthusiastic cheers, while the flag of England is nowhere seen.*

---

* It was the American flag that waved over the liberated Fenian prisoners during the recent great torch-light procession in Dublin to welcome their return. The English flag was not visible anywhere.

These are some of the outward and visible signs of the rapid spread of American influence and republican tendencies amongst the Irish people, and it is a natural result, considering the incessant intercourse, and the strong relationship existing between Ireland and America.

Year by year Ireland sends forth thousands of her people in the emigrant ships, like outcast weeds to be flung on the shores of America, a helpless crowd of crushed, dispirited, unlettered peasants; slaves and serfs who have never even known their rights as freemen, dulled by want, oppression, and despair; speaking, perhaps, no language save the ancient tongue of the primitive Celt, through which no new light of thought has flashed for a thousand years; seeing nothing, knowing nothing in all God's great universe save the two awful and irresistible forces that for them rule earth and heaven, the Landlord and the Priest.   Silent and troubled, with the scared, sad look of the hunted deer, they gather on the beach amid the wild cries of their kindred, and sail away in the exile ship, with all its unknown horrors, to the unknown land beyond the sea, as if they were passing to another life through the gates of death. But, in the next decade the children of these serfs of the desolated lives, the bewildered brain, and the darkened soul, will spring up at once to the level of the nineteenth century— ardent in purpose, fearless in word, eager for action, and filled with a glowing ambition to scale those heights which under a republic are accessible to all who have intellect and daring. The past is not forgotten, but they stand on it as on a pedestal from whence they take a wider survey of their position, and recognise the truth at last that life means something more to man than mere passive endurance of the negation of all things that build up a nation, or a human soul. They are no longer helpless, incoherent masses of ignorant and unorganized men, waifs driven by the storm-winds of despair, with only bitter memories, or vengeful hopes to guide, that, like torches held over an abyss by an uncertain hand, too often lead but to dismay and ruin.

The American Irish are the opposite of all this. They receive a soldier's training, with full privileges of freemen and citizens. They are educated and organized; important by their numbers and by that ready talent and indomitable spirit which is rapidy gaining for them the highest positions as statesmen, generals, orators, writers and journalists in the States.

The vastness of America, the gigantic enterprise, the infinite extent of her resources, the boundless wealth waiting on every side for the skilful hand and the energetic brain, have a peculiarly stimulating effect upon the multitudes who have quitted a country where energy finds no work for hand or brain, and intellect has neither honour nor reward. The lassitude and languor induced by the utter stagnation of all things at home is thrown off, and men begin to feel that if they have the gifts to win success, they have also a right to share those splendid rewards which under a monarchy are reserved almost exclusively for a favoured few, but which a republic offers freely to all. And the American Irish are now powerful enough to command success. They have become a great and mighty people in the land of their adoption —a nation greater than the nation at home. There are twice as many Irish now in America as there are in Ireland. They form a third of the population of all the great cities, and are banded together in one powerful organization by race, religion, memory, and hopes.

They have also one aim, which is to create a new era in the history of Ireland. This is the fanaticism of their lives—but they bide their time; the individual dies, the nation lives and waits. The English sneer down the idea; yet nothing will eradicate the splendid dream from the Celtic imagination that some day the Irish race will be powerful enough to re-cross the Atlantic with ships and arms and money, overthrow English rule, and annex Ireland to the great Federal Republic under the Stars and Stripes. And it must be confessed that the project is not wholly improbable or impossible should there be some new arrangement of the nationalities of the world, for America needs a stand-point in Europe; and Ireland would form a capital *Atrium* for the unresting, eternally moving masses of the American people, who, having already swept along the whole coast of the Pacific, will soon be surging across the Atlantic to seek new homes. Indeed the subject has already been openly discussed, and even a suggestion offered that America should purchase Ireland from the English Government in a peaceable, orderly way; for considering what a thorn in the flesh the Green Isle has ever been to England, the severance, it is thought, might be made without much grief on either side. Meanwhile the American Irish boast of their ten millions, all ready to pour across the Atlantic when the fitting moment comes in which they can reconstruct their ancient mother-land upon the newest Republican principles.

What may be the future of the much-tried, but ineffaceable Irish race, none can tell. No definite line of action has yet been formed, but a people who are learning, under the teaching of America, the dignity and value of human rights, are not likely to acquiesce tamely in the degraded position Ireland holds in

Europe, decay stamped on her cities and her institutions, helpless poverty on her people, who yet own a country larger, richer, and better placed for all the purposes of commerce than half the autonomous States of Europe. The Irish never forget their mother-land or give up the hope of national independence; even amongst the kind-hearted Americans they have not eaten of the Lotus that makes them forget Ithaca. But the regeneration and re-creation of Ireland will not come through "Home Rule" as understood by its present supporters and leaders, if indeed that hollow fiction is not even now wholly extinct. No one can seriously believe that the Irish nobles will ever come back to their ancient palaces, or the Queen take up her residence at Dublin Castle in a desolated city and a land of poverty, torpor, and universal decadence.

"Home Rule" with its old feudal distinctions of class and caste, is looked upon with bitter disdain by the advanced party in Irish politics, and it will never be galvanized into life again by any amount of platform platitudes.

A national convention, with supreme power over all that concerns Ireland, and control of the revenues, to be composed of members elected by universal suffrage, and secured in power for a definite time, is the idea most prominently set forth now by the American Irish. Of course a national convention without the command of the revenues of the nation would be a cheat and a delusion, for the power to make laws and decree improvements would be of little avail as long as the revenue of Ireland was poured into the treasury of another country.

The new movement will have a larger and more comprehensive aim than the mere "Repeal of the Union". The American Irish, with their bolder

views, desire to create a new system of things, not
merely to resuscitate the old, for it is not from the
shrivelled rags of effete worn-out ideas that a people
can weave the garment of the new age. The new
wine must be poured into new bottles; and a higher
object even than to increase the material prosperity
of a country is to create the moral dignity of a people,
to bring the torpid, slumbering energies of Ireland
within the influence of the powerful electric forces that
everywhere else are stirring humanity into new life.

The influence, however, must come from without.
Ireland alone and unaided has never yet accomplished
one of these great revolutions such as France, Italy
and England have had, that sweep off at once the
accumulated evils of centuries, because Ireland has no
firm organization, and therefore no power, only a
vague, nameless discontent, only a bitter sense of
wrong. One thing, however, is certain: there is a stir
in men's minds now that is a prophecy of change; the
feverish unrest that has driven the young generation
of Ireland to America will one day drive them back
again all alight with her ideas, and ready to proclaim
that in a Republic alone is to be found the true force
that emancipates the soul and the life of man.

England should have counted the cost before
compelling the Irish people to take shelter in the arms
of the mighty mother of freedom.

Yet there is nothing to alarm in the word "republic". It simply means the government of common sense
for the common good. Everyone is wearied with the old
system of things, and all long to throw off the incubus
of prejudice and routine, and fetish worship, and to
start afresh on a new career under new conditions.

We can but read the signs of the times, not strive
after vain prophecies. It is important, however, tha

those who rule the nations should study diligently the tendencies of the age throughout Europe, while to England it is of special importance to study the influences from America that are so powerfully affecting the tone of Irish thought, for Ireland may yet be the battleground where the destinies of the Empire will be decided. The American Irish are prepared for any effort, any mutation of all things, governments, and peoples and ideas, even Ireland may hope that change will bring progress. It is given to every nation once to touch the zenith, and perhaps the hour of her advancement draws nigh.

But whether the change will come through the clash of war or the peaceful organization of a great European brotherhood of freedom, none can say. The great world-movers of the future will probably cast down before they build up. The iconoclasts will precede the constructors, and the present time is emphatically iconoclastic.

All the old-world opinions, dogmas, traditions of custom and usage, all the cumbrous machinery of old-world life and political systems, have been flung into the crucible of the critics and philosophers; but what the residuum will be when the dross is eliminated, who can say.

The American Irish are eager to join this world-wide movement which is straining towards a goal set far beyond all merely local aims, or the progress of one's own race and country.

We are accustomed to think of Ireland as only a nation of five millions, according to home statistics and census reports, but, including Australia with America, the Irish may be counted at eighteen or twenty millions; and in case of some violent European complication, or of war between England and the

United States, it may be interesting to speculate on which side these millions would range themselves. Gratitude would bind them to America; they could never fight against the flag that sheltered them in their adversity, when evil laws and bitter tyranny forced them to abandon their own unhappy country; and they could scarcely be expected to show an enthusiastic desire to support England even at the sacrifice of their lives.

So tremendous a catastrophe, however, as war between England and the States will probably never happen; but revolutions may come silently and with spirit steps. Such a revolution, silent, gradual, but certain, is now going on in the Irish mind abroad and at home, and some day the new ideas will find visible expression in perhaps a higher national life than any Ireland has yet known. Education will create a new history; it is the force that above all others moulds the destiny of a people and teaches them how to utilize their chances and opportunities. Hitherto the Irish have groped blindly after their ideal, which is National Independence—this is the magic phrase that binds them together as one people all over the world, as if it symbolized a religion; and if they have striven for it through seven centuries of darkness and dis-organization, they are not likely to give it up now in this nineteenth century, when Liberty from the shores of America holds high her torch for men to read their rights by; and America has, in an especial manner, constituted herself the teacher of the Irish people. Lectures upon Irish history, poetry, oratory, and all that illustrates the genius, sufferings, wrongs and destiny of the Irish, are the most popular of all subjects throughout the States, and attract eager and sympathetic crowds; for, strange to say, these subjects have also the additional charm of novelty. The Irish people are reared upon traditions, but have little accurate knowledge of their own history, while the upper classes are notoriously ignorant of it, with the exception of a few learned academicians who study it curiously, as they do the Vedas, for mere ethnological or philological purposes.

The reason of this national ignorance is simply that Irish history is not taught in any of the schools of Ireland; not in the national schools, nor the endowed schools; nor is it included in the course at the Queen's Colleges or the Dublin University, to qualify for a degree. In Irish education, Irish history is steadily ignored by schools, academies, and colleges; a national annihilation that probably could find no counterpart in all the rest of Europe. Irish children may recite the kings of the Heptarchy, or the causes of the Punic Wars, but of the long heroic struggle of their fore-fathers against foreign domination, they are taught never a word.

Naturally the object of an alien government was to extinguish the idea of a country; to degrade and obliterate heroic memories; to brand a patriot as a traitor, and nationality as treason; and in this manner the pride, self-respect, and self-reliance of the Irish people have been slowly murdered through the centuries—for strong and noble qualities like these are only found amongst a people who are taught the dignity of nationhood, and to reverence the men of their race who have toiled, and fought, and suffered for some great idea, or some sublime word.

America, however, fully responds to the eager desire of the Irish amongst them for fuller knowledge and clearer light. Many influential journals are almost wholly devoted to Irish subjects, and the past and future of Ireland are discussed with a fearless audacity unknown here; for, as Emerson remarks, "There is a boundless freedom in the States, and people have been put to death in other countries for uttering what are but the commonplaces of American writers".

One of the best of these journals is *The Boston Pilot*, edited by an Irishman, John Boyle O'Reilly, the distinguished author of *Songs from the Southern Seas*, a series of wild, fierce tales of adventure, remarkable for startling originality of conception, nervous language, and a full flow of sonorous harmonies in the versification. Another journal of considerable critical ability, *The New York Nation*, is also edited by an Irishman, Mr. Godkin, son of the author of *Ireland and her Churches*, and other works. *The Irish World*, the favourite organ of the ultra-democratic party, has a fiercer inspiration, and openly advocates an armed invasion of Ireland, and the redistribution of all the confiscated estates. This journal is indeed so violently anti-English, and the illustrations are so bitterly sarcastic on the English Court (although with none of the revolting ribaldry permitted to appear in London in papers like the *Tomahawk*), that recently it has been stopped at the Irish post office, and the priesthood discourage its circulation amongst the people. It is, however, extremely popular with the extreme section of the American Irish, and is held to be a true exponent of their views.

Amongst the many works issued by the American press on Irish subjects, the most recent, and by far the most important, is the History of the Successive Confiscation of Ireland, by Mr. Amory, including lists of the families whose estates were seized and divided amongst the English adventurers.* The work has

* *The Transfer of Erin*, by Thomas C. Amory. Lippencott and Co., Philadelphia, 1877.

excited great attention in America, for descendants of all these families may be found in the States, and they are proud of their kinship with the old historic clans.*

Mr. Amory, the author, an American of distinguished position, influence, and wealth, whose opinion is of the highest value, writes with much kindly feeling of the Irish, yet with fairness and moderation, while he states the truth boldly at the same time, with respect to English policy, as only an American may dare to do. "If Ireland," he says, "still remains turbulent and disaffected, the fault is due to England, who never strove to gain the love of the people, but crushed, and despoiled, and exterminated in place of affiliating. Had Irishmen," he continues, "been left lords of their own lands, and not made bondsmen to strangers, they would have been the honour and safety of the united realm, and proved themselves, as they are in America, an intelligent, thrifty, law-abiding, brave, generous, and noble-hearted people." And when the Irish have shown themselves so worthy of freedom, he considers it "base and unjust in the highest degree for English writers to pursue them across the Atlantic, casting obloquy on their nation, their history, and their traditions, with the sole aim apparently of lowering them in the eyes of the people who shelter and protect them".

In the interest, therefore, of fair play he undertook the work "to show the true nature of English rule from which sprang all the evils of Irish destiny". And he has accomplished his task with great ability. Every page shows careful and extensive reading, and patient

---

* An immense interest has been recently manifested in America on the subject of family history. Since the close of the war people have had little to do, and so have taken to heraldry, and we may soon expect a Columbian King-at-arms, and an American Debrett.

study of the involved and complicated details of Irish history, along with a generous, high-spirited feeling towards Ireland, that contrasts very favourably with the usual tone of English writers on the same subject. In the early portion of the History, he chiefly follows "the Four Masters," but he has also amassed material from many other sources, ancient and modern, so that his volume is really a condensed history of Ireland down to the time of Elizabeth, when the last gleam of independent sovereignty died out with the submission of the great O'Neill, after a ceaseless war of four hundred years between the two races. A second volume will tell the story of Irish confiscations from James I to Cromwell and William of the Boyne; after which the gloom of the penal laws settled on the country, and the Irish had no more land to be confiscated, nor even a legal right to hold any land on their own soil. "For a far less amount of wrong," Mr. Amory remarks, "the Americans cast off the English yoke for ever, and proclaimed independence."

The early portion of Irish history is passed over slightly, for there were no confiscations prior to the Norman Invasion. The land belonged to the Clan, and the goods of life were abundant and shared by all alike. The condition of the Irish people was better a thousand years ago than it is now; the progress of civilization makes the rich richer, but the poor poorer.* They seem to have lived happily in those primitive days with music and song and cosherings and feastings,

---

* A thousand years ago the people of Ireland had their share in the cattle of the plains, the salmon of the rivers, and the deer of the forest; now the railroads carry off all the produce of land and rivers for export. The great proprietors in consequence grow wealthy, but the peasants are reduced to the level of a root-eating people, and never taste meat but twice a year—at Christmas and Easter.

where they drank at their banquets of "the best seven sorts of wine", and never a care troubled them save an occasional brush with the Danes, or with each other, to keep their shields bright and their swords keen. Nor were they deficient in artistic culture; their golden diadems, torques, bracelets, and other personal ornaments were costly and splendid, and evinced a skill in workmanship rarely equalled in this day. Like the Greeks, they prized highly personal gifts and their kings were chosen for their stature, strength, and beauty. Courage they esteemed as one of the noblest virtues, and victory the highest glory. "What do you desire?" asked Saint Bridget of a great chief. "Shall I pray that the crown may never depart from your race, and that your soul may find rest in heaven?" "I care not for heaven," he answered, "of which I know nothing, but for long life in this world, in which I greatly delight, and for victory over my enemies." And Saint Patrick, having questioned the king on the eve of battle, "Which will you have—for my prayers are powerful—defeat to-day and heaven for ever, or victory and hell?" received the emphatic answer, "Hell to all eternity; so the victory is mine to-day in the battle!"

When the Normans came, the Irish were no rude barbarians, as some English writers have endeavoured to represent them. They had a Christian civilization of seven centuries; a learned priesthood, honoured throughout Europe; colleges for instruction, the resort of many Saxon princes; musicians eminent in their art above all others; and a code of wise just laws, including evidences of much tender feeling towards the weak and helpless. Even in the pagan time a queen of Ireland erected a hospital near her own royal residence for the sick and those wounded in battle, and called it "The

House of Sorrow". The many stately abbeys, the
sculptured crosses, the illuminated manuscripts (which
to the Normans seemed the work of angels) attest their
wonderful sense of symmetry and beauty, and their
reverence for all things pertaining to religion; while
evidences of a still older art and culture exist in those
mystic towers which Giraldus Cambrensis gazed upon
with awe and wonder above six centuries ago, and
which, happily, though volumes have been written on
the subject, still remain inscrutable, for nothing could
be more revolting to the imaginative mind than the
satisfactory solution of a world-old mystery.

Further back, even in the very night of time, are the
sepulchres of the Boyne and the Cyclopean Temple
of New Grange, relics of the same mighty race that
dwelt on the Argive plain, and were the Cyclopean
builders of mycenae. Rude in art, but powerful in
strength, their tombs stand to this day in all their
awful and majestic grandeur in Ireland as in Greece,
memorials of the great, silent race, that had no
literature and no alphabet, but whose colossal symbols
of expression were temples and tombs.

The Celts in many things had a strong affinity with
the Greeks, the highest honours were given to learning
and poetry, and their music had the same subtle power
ascribed to the Dorian measure which had "such
strange influence over the human soul, that the bards
were often summoned to heal feuds by their divine
harmony".

A people of this sensitive temperament, proud,
passionate, and warlike, accustomed to think greatly
of their race who had owned the soil for nearly two
thousand years before the coming of the Normans,
and had never endured the yoke of the Cæsars, nor
the presence of a foreign enemy, save the pirate Danes

of the coasts, was ill-fitted to bear the hard insulting tyranny of English rule. The stolid Saxons had a different temperament, they were rapidly crushed and humbled and made the serfs of their Norman masters; and after a while they patiently accepted their fate and became the traders and toilers and factory hands of the Empire, no man pitying them. It was evident that nature meant them for a destiny of inferiority, for a servile race, and so they have remained ever since, emphatically "the lower classes" of England.

The Celts, on the contrary, with their Greek nature, love glory, and beauty, and distinction, everything that is free and splendid, but they hate toil and despise trade. They were made for warriors and orators, for a life of excitement and daring, lit by swift impulses, fast and fiery as electric flashes. They will do anything for love or fame. They adore a hero, but they will never tamely submit to coercion, injustice, and a position of inferiority, like the apathetic, dull-brained Saxon.

It would indeed be impossible to find natures more entirely antagonistic than the Saxon and the Celt. The English live under method and rule, laboriously and industriously, without excitement or ambition, and will even bear oppression, so as a chance of gain comes with it. They will manufacture muskets for their own country, or for the foreign army that fights against England, with equal readiness, and dispassionate commercial calm; and they will shout for war with the Turk or the Christian, or against them, not for the sake of God, but for the sake of cotton.

But of all races the Celt is the most easily led by the affections. If the people believe that their popular hero really loves Ireland, they would sacrifice their lives for him. The English are grateful for benefits to self, the Irish are grateful for sympathy with their country. When they say of a man, "He died for Ireland", the voice is low and tender, as if they spoke of the passion of Christ.

The great mistake of England was not trying to gain the love of this people. The Irish demand some visible personal object for their homage and devotion, but England's rule was only known to them through cruel Acts of Parliament, and to her demand for "gratitude" they might have answered—

"We, for all our good things have at your hands— Death, barrenness, child slaughter, curses, cares, Sea leaguer, and land shipwreck, which of these— Which shall we first give thanks for"?

The Irish are naturally loyal, with an almost oriental abnegation of self, to those they love; but the English never cultivated their affection, and never comprehended the deeply reverential Irish nature, so full of passionate fanaticism that sympathy with their ideal, whatever that may be, whether in politics or religion, is more to them than if gold were showered upon their path; but as they never received sympathy or affection, but only taunts, insults, and penal laws, the history of Ireland, from the fatal year 1172 to the present hour, is the saddest in Europe.

Yet, the first invaders conquered more through love than war. The Normans were a fine, brave, high-spirited race, one of the leonine races with firm noses, as Victor Hugo describes them, destined to conquer. They intermarried rapidly with the royal families of Ireland, and thus immense estates passed into their hands, many of which are held by their descendants to this day. The five daughters of Isabel, granddaughter of King Dermot MacMurrough, had each a county for her dower; they all wedded English nobles, and it is remarkable that to this line can be traced all the highest names in the English peerage, the royal family of England, and, through the Stuarts, all the leading crowned heads of Europe.

The Norman Irish, the descendants of these mixed marriages, grew into a splendid and powerful race, the Geraldines at their head. Queen Elizabeth came of this blood through her mother and the Ormonds, indeed, Mr. Hepworth Dixon imputes the fascinations of Anna Boleyn to this Irish strain; and the Irish gradually came to love these Norman nobles who lived amongst them, adopted their speech and dress, and often fought with the Clans against England. But these strong bonds of friendship soon excited the jealousy of the English kings, and it is a singular fact that the first coercion laws in Ireland were enacted to break this amity between the two races. Marriage was strictly forbidden with the Irish, and fosterage for the children grew so fond of their foster kindred, that they often refused to leave them, and renouncing allegiance to England, adopted the Irish mode of life and dress. But no laws were found adequate to prevent intermarriage. Even Spencer, the poet, when he came over to receive his three thousand acres of the forfeited estates, took to wife an Irish girl, whose portrait he has sketched so prettily in the "Epithalamium"; and all Cromwell's troopers, when they settled down with their land warrants, married Irishwomen, despite of the severest penalties. Then a new danger alarmed England, for the children of these marriages spoke nothing but Irish, and complaints were made by the officials that the English tongue was almost dying out in Ireland; further efforts were made in consequence to force the English settlers to put away their Irish wives, but in vain.   Thus a second mixed race sprang up in Ireland, still known as "the Cromwellian Irish", strong Protestants, but Liberal in politics, and rather Republican in theory. Meanwhile the Irish disdained to use the language of the invaders, or adopt their dress, for "the tribes of Erin ever hated foreign modes". The English kings sometimes sent over presents of costly robes to the great chieftains, but they refused to wear them; and Shane O'Neill appeared at the Court of Queen Elizabeth in the long flowing yellow mantle, brooched with gold, after the Irish fashion, and addressed her Majesty in Irish, which she was ungracious enough to say resembled "the howling of a dog".   When asked to confer in English with the Commissioners, he replied indignantly, "What! shall an O'Neill writhe his mouth in clattering English?"   The husband of Grana-Uaile, a De Burgho, could speak French, and Latin, and Irish, but no English; and one frequently reads in the annals of some Norman noble, who swore brotherhood with an Irish chieftain, and assumed the Irish dress, and Irish speech, in sign of friendship.

In order therefore to crush more completely the tendency to union between the two races, drawn together by sentiments of chivalry and love, a policy of the most insulting degradation was adopted towards the Irish of the Pale.   They were forced to give up their old historic names, and assume hideous and unmeaning surnames, from colours, as black, white, grey, green, brown; or from fishes, as salmon, cod, haddock, plaice, and every other stupid appellation that malice could invent, and by which the old associations of noble descent might be obliterated. They were also excluded from all places of trust and honour; the son had to follow his father's trade, lest by some chance he should rise in the social scale; and at all times it seems to have been held a praiseworthy act to kill an Irishman, without let or hindrance, fear of law, or punishment of the slayer. The Norman nobles who sided with the Clans were also persecuted, and great portions of their estates were given over to a new lot of English colonists less friendly to the Irish. The Geraldines especially, being the most powerful, were treated with most severity. In the reign of Henry VIII, six nobles of the Geraldines were executed in London for aiding rebellion amongst the Irish, but even this bitter vengeance could not quench their national zeal. From Silken Thomas to the fated and interesting Lord Edward Fitzgerald, the great house of Kildare has always been on the side of the Irish nation.

The war of Races lasted without intermission for four hundred years, dating from the invasion, until the fall of O'Neill, Earl of Tyrone, the last independent prince of Ulster.* Then followed the still fiercer war of religions, which has not even yet ended. Queen Elizabeth resolved that the Irish should become Protestant, and burnings, massacres, and devastation were the persuasive means employed.

All who would not conform were driven from their homes and left to perish in the bogs and woods where they tried to find a shelter. All the South was confiscated and divided amongst a set of Protestant English adventurers. The Irish were cast forth to die and the horrible work of destruction went on until even the Queen complained that she would soon reign only over ashes and corpses. Spencer, the poet, has left a vivid description of the state of Ireland at that

---

* The Reverend C. P. Meehan has graphically described this memorable epoch of Irish history in his admirable volume entitled *The Flight of the Earls*.

time. He describes the land as "the fairest upon earth", but the people wandered about like ghosts from the grave, houseless and starving, and all the roads were strewn with the unburied dead. When King James came to the throne the Irish had a gleam of hope. He was a Stuart of the line of their ancient kings, and they looked for tenderness at his hands for the sake of his Catholic mother; but the hope was vain. The war of religions waxed fiercer, and the persecution was more bitter and cruel. Queen Elizabeth had confiscated the South; King James confiscated the North, and handed over the fishful rivers and broad lands of Ulster to the worshipful Fishmongers of London, who rejoice in their possession even unto this day. And again, massacres, burnings, and devastation were the means employed to get rid of the unhappy natives of the soil. It was not wonderful that a terrible vendetta should be the result. In the memorable year 1641 the Irish rose *en masse*, headed by Lord Maguire, Earl of Enniskillen, with the avowed object of sweeping all the English out of the island at once, seizing Dublin Castle, and proclaiming a national independent government. But the project failed, as all projects against English power have failed in Ireland. Lord Maguire was captured and brought over to London for trial. He was but twenty-six (the leaders of revolutions are all young), and he met his fate with the calmness of a martyr for religion. When they teased him with taunts upon Romish doctrines, and advice to abjure them, he only answered, "I pray you, gentlemen, let me have peace that I may pray". He earnestly pleaded to be tried by his peers in deference to his rank, and to be beheaded in place of being hung, these requests were denied; and having been degraded from his title of

Lord Enniskillen, which afterwards was conferred upon one of the Cole family, he was drawn on a sledge from the Tower through London, and on to Tyburn, where being removed into a cart he kneeled down and prayed awhile, and so was executed.* The war of religions went on with still increasing bitterness during the republican period between the Irish, who held for King Charles, and the parliamentary forces, until Cromwell himself at last appeared upon the scene, and stifled Royalists and Catholics alike in a bath of blood. South and North had already been confiscated. Cromwell completed the work by confiscating all the rest of Ireland. His policy was extermination, and this he carried out with a ruthless ferocity that has made his name eternally abhorred in Ireland. "The curse of Cromwell on you" is the bitterest malediction a peasant can utter even at this day.

The Irish were the Canaanites to be hewed down branch and root. Had the nation had but one neck he would have struck it off. The priests were massacred by hundreds, the nobles were driven into exile, the women and children were sold in thousands as slaves to the West Indian planters. The whole of the land was seized, and five million acres were parcelled out by lot to his troops in payment of their arrears of pay.

The bleakest portion of Connaught alone was reserved for the remnant of the Irish people amidst the wild, treeless mountains of the West, and thither the fugitives were driven during all the rigours of winter,

---

* An interesting novel founded on the rising of 1641 entitled *Tully Castle*, by Mr. Magennis, of Fermanagh, has recently appeared. The hero is Lord Maguire, and the trial scene and his tragic death are drawn with much power and minute accuracy of detail.

with orders not to approach within five miles of the
sea under penalty of death—the object being to shut
up the last survivors of the Irish nation from all
intercourse with the world, and if possible to extirpate
them wholly by famine and sickness.

One should read this tragic tale of the uprooting of
a nation in Mr. Prendergast's great historic work
The Cromwellian Settlement of Ireland.* No nation ever
endured greater horrors, and no people but the Ir'sh
could have survived them. The land remained un-
tilled, the cattle and corn were destroyed, and food
had to be imported from Wales for Cromwell's
soldiery. A court-martial sat in St. Patrick's Cathedral, and all delinquents who refused to go to
Connaught were hanged, with a placard on the breast,
for not transplanting. The corpses of the slain and the
famine struck were flung into the ditches; multitudes
perished from want, and the roads were covered with
the unburied dead. The wolves came down from the
mountains in such numbers to seize their prey, that
travelling became dangerous because of them. Then
a price was set on the wolves and on the men who still
wandered about the woods and bogs near their
ancient homes—five pounds for the skin of a wolf, ten
pounds for the head of an Irishman, even twenty
pounds if he were distinguished; still the heads did not
come in fast enough, and a free pardon was then
offered to any Irishman who killed another and
brought his head to claim the reward.

At length Parliament interfered, with a suggestion
that it were better not to extirpate the whole nation,
but to leave some to till the ground, as the commis-

---

* One of the most valuable contributions which this age has given to Irish
history, and perfectly trustworthy, being compiled from authentic sources and
State papers.

sioners reported that four-fifths of the richest land lay
waste and uninhabited.

The English had now been governing Ireland for
five hundred years, and this was the result. The
accession of James II, however, promised better times.
He was a Stuart and a Catholic, and the Irish always
clung with fatal fondness to the Stuart race, as being
of their own blood. But loyalty had no better fate
than disaffection. They had leagued with Spain for
the sake of King Charles; they now leagued with
France for the sake of King James. Cromwell
avenged the first, and William of Orange the second
attempt to support English royalty by foreign arms;
and after the decisive conflict of 1688 a deeper
darkness settled upon Ireland. The policy of Elizabeth and her successors was *confiscation*; that of
Cromwell *extermination*, but the policy of King William,
or rather of his Parliament, was *degradation*, for the
penal laws meant social and moral death; and
statesmen then sedulously set themselves the task of
debasing a whole people below the level of humanity.
As a hero, William loved all heroism; and the splendid
valour of the Irish, their devotion to their king, their
country, and their faith filled him with wonder and
admiration. "Give them any terms they ask," he
wrote to his generals at Limerick. And when twenty
thousand of the best and bravest in Ireland went forth
from the surrendered city and ranged themselves
under the French flag, to pass from thence into the
armies of his hereditary foe, how bitterly he regretted
that such men should be driven into exile, or degraded
to slaves if they remained at home. Earnestly he
offered them everything men naturally desire—rank,
wealth, a position as high in his army as they held in
their own, if they would only enter his service. But

the Irish heeded not; they kneeled down reverently to
kiss the Irish soil for a last farewell, and then passed on
to the ships amidst such lamentations as never were
heard before in Ireland, and sailed away from their
native land never to behold it more.*
The laws of William's Parliament were cruel, but
those of Queen Anne were ferocious.   No other nation
ever invented a code so fitted to destroy both soul and
body.   The son was set against the father, brother
against brother, for the law decreed that the informer
and betrayer should be rewarded with the estates and
property of his victim.

During the whole of the eighteenth century this
atrocious code was endured by the Irish without any
open revolt; but at last the bitter indignation of the
people burst forth in the great rebellion of 1798—
a movement, strange to say, which originated with
the Presbyterians of Ulster, the descendants of the
Scotch settlers of King James.   Their object at first
was simply to repeal the infamous penal laws, but
gradually the organization became republican under
French influence, and the leadership of the fated Lord
Edward Fitzgerald.

How the rebellion was put down is still fresh in the
minds of the people, for the generation is not yet
extinct whose fathers witnessed the atrocities practised.

The pitch cap was the favourite amusement of the
English soldiery; piles of these caps were kept in
readiness at the barracks, and when filled with
burning pitch one was pressed tightly on the head of
the victim, who, half-blinded and maddened by the

---

* *The History of the Irish Brigade*, by Mr. O'Callaghan, gives a full account of
the fate and fortune of these distinguished Irishmen and their descendants.
Many of them founded noble families on the Continent, as the MacMahons
of France, the O'Donnells of Spain, the Nugents, Taaffes, and O'Reillys of
Austria, and many others.

agony, was then turned out to run the gauntlet of his savage tormentors until he dropped dead amidst their shouts of ferocious laughter.

Gunpowder was rubbed into the hair and then set on fire; the ears were cut off; priests and gentlemen of station were half hung to extort information. Irish vengeance in return was often fierce and terrible, but deliberate torture does not seem to have been practised at the rebel camp, and many impulsive acts of generosity in saving life are recorded of the insurgents.*

At length '98 was put down; seventy thousand Irish lay dead, but the penal laws remained unchanged. The Irish Parliament at last began seriously to consider the disaffected state of the nation. Splendid men of genius and high purpose rose up to denounce wrong, injustice, and tyranny; and the most magnificent advocacy of a people's rights ever uttered was heard in the Irish Parliament just before its fall. But the answer England gave to the noble appeal of the Irish patriots was brief and decisive; she simply annihilated the Parliament, and the voices of the prophets of freedom were heard no more.

The degradation of Ireland was now complete. After the Union, the palaces of the nobles were left desolate; wealth, spirit, enterprise, all the brilliancy of social and intellectual life vanished from the capital;

---

* On the day the rebels entered Wexford, the rector, Archdeacon Elgee, assembled a few of his parishioners in the church to partake of the sacrament together, knowing that a dreadful death awaited them. On his return, the rebels were already forcing their way into his house; they seized him, and the pikes were already at his breast, when a man stepped forth and told of some great act of kindness which the Archdeacon had shown to his family.

In an instant the feeling changed, and the leader gave orders that the Archdeacon and all that belonged to him should be held safe from harm. A rebel guard was set over his house and not a single act of violence was permitted.

But that same evening all the leading gentlemen of the town were dragged from their houses and piked by the rebels upon Wexford Bridge.

the various trades died out one by one; literature became extinct; the publishing trade, once so vigorous and flourishing, almost entirely disappeared; the currents of thought and energy set to London, and have continued to flow there ever since, draining the life-blood of Ireland to fill the veins of England, and all that makes a nation great and strong and self-respecting was annihilated.

With splendid eloquence the great orators Grattan, Plunkett, Bushe, denounced the evils of the Union, and their burning words have fed the flame of disaffection to it ever since, but with little result. Concessions, indeed, were made at last, but they came tardily and grudgingly. It is only within a few years that Catholics have been admitted to social and political equality with Protestants—the Catholics of to-day are the children of the bond-slaves of yesterday; they were born in fetters, and the concessions of England, as they generally do, came too late for gratitude from the embittered hearts of a long oppressed people. But the Irish themselves are also much to blame; their efforts are never organized with the strength and unanimity that produce great results. Religious animosity is the upas-tree perpetually distilling its fatal poison upon every broad and liberal project of national advancement. The great French Revolution overthrew the feudal tyranny of a thousand years. Freedom was purchased with much blood, still it was gained; but Irish revolt against oppression only strengthened the fetters; the love of liberty that originated the movement soon degenerated into a rabid hatred of Race and Creed, and no good fruit has ever grown upon that evil tree.

Other nations have had their seven years' war, or thirty years' war, but Ireland has carried on an utterly unavailing war of seven hundred years, and even yet scarcely recognizes the truth that to raise Ireland to the splendid position in the Empire to which she is entitled, there should be a clear, dignified programme of measures, to which all noble natures could say Amen, and the united action of a whole people to obtain their fulfilment. Disaffection is not an evil where wrongs exist, it is the lever of progress, but incoherent disaffection only scatters and weakens the energies of a people. This is painfully evident in Ireland at the present time, where a mournful and hopeless stagnation rests upon all things; the professions languish, the nobility are absentees, the commercial classes are merely agents for the English manufacturers; there is no stimulus to work, no career, no rewards for intellect, no wealth to support art or literature; and every young man of education and culture must look abroad for a fair open for his gifts, and be content to leave Ireland to her destiny as a mere cattle-pen for England, and a co-operative store to sell her surplus goods.

The ignorance of English statesmen, also, respecting the needs, the history, and even the existing condition of the people, has been highly prejudicial to the country. No large, liberal measures are ever thought of as a remedy for acknowledged "disaffection". Complaint is answered by a coercion bill, and the only remedial act is to proclaim a district. The present Prime Minister has never visited Ireland, and knows so little of the country he governs—a country that has been devastated, plundered and three times confiscated, and reduced by want and famine from eight millions to five millions during the last thirty years— that he imputes all the discontent of the Irish solely to their position beside "the melancholy ocean".

English statesmen might study with advantage the mode by which the Greeks, the great colonizers of the ancient world, gained the love of all peoples. Like England, the Greeks carried on extensive commerce with many strange nations, but they never sought to exterminate; they humanized. Their trade swept by many shores, but not to destroy, or burn, or ravage. They opened bazaars, they built temples, they planted corn, and erected factories. If they wanted land they took it, but civilized the people, and drew them up into their own higher civilization; they gave their wine and oil for the corn and flax of the stranger, but still more, the wine and oil of their own richly gifted intellects, and they freely intermarried with the foreign peoples, especially with the Celts, between whom and the Greeks there was ever a strong affinity of nature, temperament, and character.

So they passed on in ceaseless migration, founding states wherever they landed, but leaving every state to be self-governed, though bound to Greece by the strong bonds of love and gratitude.

Above all people, the Greeks seem to have been endowed with the gift of personal fascination; the English as a nation have none of it, though capable of splendid acts of individual generosity. The colonists were proud to be called Greek, and felt a pride in the triumphs of the Greek name; but in Ireland the word *Sassenach* inspired only fear, and dread, and hatred. The English strove to crush the mind of the subject race, knowing that culture is power, but the Greeks gave civilization and refinement, art, science, and philosophy. They conquered by their divine gifts, and the colonists in return glorified Greece by their genius; wherever the Greeks passed they left a trail of light, but England a trail of blood.

England never had a divine idea in the treatment of nationalities, least of all in Ireland.

Nothing grand or noble in policy was ever thought of to lift the people to their true height. Self was the only motive power; greed of land, greed of wealth the only aim; the lust of gold everywhere, the love of God nowhere; spoliation and insult the only policy; the result being that no nation has ever been so unsuccessful in gaining the love of subject states as England. It is told of the Emperor Aurelian that having decreed the destruction of the city of Tyana, the philosopher Apollonius appeared to him in a dream and said—"Aurelian, if you would conquer, abstain from the destruction of cities; Aurelian, if you would reign, abstain from the blood of the innocent; Aurelian, if you would be loved, be just and merciful". It is strange that royal races so seldom seem to understand that their only claim to loyalty is in so far as they promote the good of the people. In the government of a nation there should be one thing steadfast—Right; one thing ever sacred—Truth; one thing ever manifested—Love; but this is a gospel seldom preached by statesmen. The prosperity of a country means to them its commercial value, not the moral elevation of the souls committed to their charge.

But no doubt there is also some instinctive antagonism, or deficiency of sympathy between English and Irish nature, to account for the eternal war of races, religions, and temperaments through so many centuries. The English are half made of iron like their soil; robust, stern, steadfast in purpose, without illusions, without dreams, without reverence; but in the soft, relaxing air of Ireland, the energies of the people are only stirred fitfully, like the sudden storms of their own mountain lakes. There is no persistent force, and the utter stagnation of life, the absence of all motive to exertion forces the people to live in the past, or the future, rather than energetically in the present. They are always dreaming that to-morrow will give them all they require, for to-day gives them nothing. The English, on the contrary, in their full overflowing life of the present, have no time for vain lamentations over the past. What English-man now cares for the devastations of the Common-wealth, even with its solemn tragedy of a king's death, or for the deadly struggle of Guelph and Stuart? The exports of cotton and the price of corn are more to them than the story of all the dynasties since the Conquest. They never loved any of their kings. They have no popular idol in all their history. No great historic fact has become part of the national life. No lofty aspiration inspires their oratory. They live wholly in the sensuous and the actual. The Irish live on dreams and prayer. Religion and country are the two words round which their lives revolve.

The frame-work, also, is different in which their souls are set. The factory smoke is so thick in England the people cannot see heaven. In their hard industrial life their eyes are never lifted from toil; in their ears is only the rush of the wheels and the stroke of the hammer; and the air they breathe is the poison dust of a world-wide commerce. But the Irish, without manufactures or commerce, or anything to do save tend the cattle for English food, can at least live, as it were, in the visible presence of God, in the free enjoyment of lake and river, and mountain unsullied by the smoke of labour. The world above is a reality to the Irish peasant. No people have more intense faith in the unseen. It is their religious temperament, so childlike in its simplicity and trust, that alone makes their life of privation endurable, and enables them to meet all sorrows, even death itself, with the pathetic fatalism expressed in the phrase so often heard from peasant lips, "It was the will of God."

The round, stolid English head, and pale, cold eyes, denote the nation of practical aims, a people made for commerce and industry; while the small oval head of the Celt, and deep, passionate eyes, denote a people made for religion and art; and, therefore, the greatest mistake ever made by England was the endeavour to force the Reformation on a people like the Irish. Protestantism, without art, or beauty, or ritual, or symbol, or reverence, suited the self-asserting, dogged egotism of the English.   The right of private judgment means to them simply that every man is as good a udge as the parson, or better.   The stolid parishioner pays the clergymen to do a certain duty, as he pays the doctor and the lawyer, but no sanctity surrounds the Protestant priesthood.

The Reformation was a genuine outcome of Saxon nature; a rude revolt against grace, refinement, the beautiful, and the mystic; a cold appeal to the lowest level of the understanding; not a sublime and un-questioning acceptance of an awful revelation from the lips of a consecrated priesthood.

Both in religion and politics the Irish need the visible symbol.   Their ideal must be impersonated in some form they can reverence, worship and love. What sad Irish mother, with her half-famished children round her in their miserable cabin, could bear with life day by day without the infinite trust in the Divine Mother who, she believes, is watching over and pitying her?   What could Protestantism with its hard scholastic dogmas do for such a people?   In place of the Divine Mother, the solemn emotional ritual, the

mystic symbols of altar and cross, they were offered
the abstractions of theology in the Thirty-nine Articles;
while, with the blasphemous boast that it was the work
of God, their stately and beautiful abbeys were
plundered and made desolate, where, not self, but the
abnegation of self, was the pure ideal of the high
ascetic life, and in their place were set up the bare,
bleak, whitewashed parish churches.

The Irish, however, found no comfort in the Thirty-
nine Articles, and would not enter the parish
churches. They preferred to die, and so thousands of
them were slaughtered with their priests, and the rest
were degraded to pariahs in their own land; still
through all the fires of persecution, they clung to their
ancient faith with a fervour that makes the devotion
of the Irish to their creed and priesthood during the
bitter martyrdom of three hundred years, one of the
most touching chapters in all human history.

But new paths opened through the darkness. God
has many agents by which peoples and nations are
driven forth to be trained and educated by strong,
fresh influences. They seem evil at first, yet it is by
such means—war, pestilence, and famine—that the
human race has been made to drift on, ever westward,
during the last three thousand years.

America is the great teacher of the nations, and her
lessons will eventually lead the world. In '93
American ideas overthrew the thousand-year-old
Monarchy of France, and they will probably overthrow the monarchies of all Europe in time. The
next great movement in Ireland will not be a rising
of the peasantry against the police, it will be as a part
of the European struggle of the masses against a
dominant minority. Lines, like hidden electrical
wires, or republican feeling, traverse unseen the

whole soil of Ireland; a touch will wake them into action.

What the unknown future may bring, none can predict, but another half century will witness assuredly a new order of things in society and politics. One can hear already the low murmur of the advancing waves of change, and in the endless sacrifice to obtain the autonomy of Ireland—that natural right of self-government which, as Mr. Gladstone says, belongs to all peoples.

Peril and danger may be in the way, but they accept and brave all consequences.

> "They wait beneath the furnace blast
>   The pangs of transformation;
> Not painlessly doth God recast,
>   Or mould anew a nation."

Meanwhile England, all-powerful England, may effect a social revolution peacefully and without any danger to the integrity of the Empire, if wise and just measures are organized in time for the true advance-ment and prosperity of Ireland; and the Irish people, in return, will stand faithfully by England in those hours of peril which seem gathering in clouds of darkness upon the horizon, and threatening dangers which only a united empire can meet and overcome.

INDEX

Calderon, Philip, 178
Callan, Margaret, 35
Cambridge History of English Literature, 163
Campbell, Lady Archibald, 176
Carleton, William, 17, 22
Carlisle, Lord, 65
Carlyle, Mrs., 129
Carlyle, Thomas, 30, 31, 127, 129, 166
Catholic Encyclopædia, 38
Chant, Mrs. Ormiston, 152
Chelsea, 166, 168, 169, 170–1, 177, 182–3, 186, 190–193
Christiana, 47
Cigar Club, 107
Civil List Pension, 142, 183
Clarendon, Lord, 34, 35
Clodd, Edward, 105
Coercion Bill, 21
Compendium of Irish Biography, 102
Cook, Eliza, 40, 64
Cook, John, 64
Cooper, Edith, 109
Copenhagen, 46, 47
Corday, Charlotte, 156
Corelli, Marie, 118, 123, 140, 152
Corkran, Henrietta, 77, 182, 194
Court Guide, 66
Courtney, W. L., 152
Covent Garden Theatre, 13
Craik, Mrs., 154
Croker, J. W., 155
Cunninghame, Lady Fairly, 151
Currie, Lady, 151

Daily News, 35, 140
Daily Telegraph. 106, 130
Daniel Deronda, 139

Davidson, John, 63
Davis, John, 166
Davis, Thomas, 17, 26, 64, 103
Denmark, 47
De Vere, Aubrey, 22, 54, 55, 56, 62, 163
Dictionary of National Biography, 135
Dillon, John, 17
Disraeli, Benjamin, 137, 138, 149
Dixie, Lady Florence, 131
Douglas, Lord Alfred, 74, 120, 125
Dowden, Professor, 142
Downing, Ellen, 27
Drury Lane Theatre, 13, 113
Dublin Book of Irish Verse, 64
Dublin Castle, 33, 65, 164
Dublin City, 43–48
Dublin Review, 75
Dublin University Magazine, 63, 75, 109, 133
Dufferin, Lord, 67
Duffy, Charles Gavan, 15–42, 63, 146, 163, 166, 188
Dumas, Alexandre, 39
Dunsink Observatory, 58

Elgee, Archdeacon, 12, 30, 66
Elgee, Charles, 12, 13, 15
Elgee, Jane Francesca (see Lady Wilde)
Eliot, George, 138, 139
Ellis, Havelock, 71
"Ellis, John Fenshaw", 23, 24, 26, 28, 29
Endymion, 12, 177
Epstein, Jacob, 122

Faithful, Emily, 143
Fane, Lady Augusta, 121
Faucit, Helen, 46, 114

Kean, Charles, 178
Kean, Edmund, 13
Kelly, Eva Mary, 27
Kemble, Charles, 191
Kemble, John Philip, 13
Kensal Green Cemetery, 190, 191
Keogh, John, 103
Kernahan, Coulson, 120
Kiel, 46
Kilkenny Archæological Journal, 104
Kingsbury, Miss, 12
Kingsford, Anna, 121
Knight, Olivia, 27
Knights of St. Patrick, 65
Kottabos, 174, 175
Kroemar, Baron von, 47

Lady's Pictorial, 144
"Lady Windermere's Fan", 159
Lamartine, Alphonse, 135, 142
Lamb, Charles, 159
Lancet, 66, 97, 99, 101
Landon, Letitia, 40, 64
Langtry, Mrs., 120, 124
Larcom, Colonel, 52, 61
Larcom, Mrs., 52, 61
Lecky, W. E. H., 16, 19, 109
Lee, Elizabeth, 175
Leslie, Mrs. Frank, 166, 167
Letters to New Ireland, 180
Leighton, Lord, 113
Lever, Charles, 43
Life of Sir William Rowan Hamilton, 51
Linton, Mrs. Lynn, 141
Liverpool, 46
Livingstone, Dr., 143
Locksley Hall, 54
Londonderry, Lord, 140
London Review, 97
Lough Corrib, 44

Love and Cabal, 41
Lover, Samuel, 19
Lucas, Frederick, 38
Lyon, Ponsonby, 121
Lytton, Lord, 138, 139

Maccarthy, Denis, 17
Macdermott, Martin, 15, 27, 64
Mackay, Charles, 97
MacNeven, Thomas, 17
Macready, W. C., 13
McCarthy, Justin, 27
McClure, Sir Robert, 12
Mahaffy, J. P., 68, 69, 75
Mangan, Clarence, 17, 22
Martin, Sir Theodore, 46, 114
Martineau, Harriet, 140
Mathers, Helen, 161
Maturin, Charles, 12
Maxwell, W. B., 173
Meinhold, William, 135
Melmoth the Wanderer, 13
Menken, Adah Isaacs, 64
Meredith, George, 113
Merrion Square, 49, 65, 68–76, 78, 81, 91, 100, 106, 114, 168–169, 188
Middlemarch, 139, 140
Miles, Frank, 120
Modern Review, 105, 106
Monahan, Chief Justice, 85–95
Moore, George, 42, 160, 166, 183
Moore, George Henry, 73
Moore, Tom, 19, 22, 40, 137, 139
Morgan, Augustus de, 52
Morgan, Lady, 143, 184, 185
Morris, Lady, 111
Mount Jerome Cemetery, 101, 103
Mulready, William, 191
Mulrenin, Bernard, 65, 78
Munday, Luther, 121

INDEX

Wilde, Ralph, 42
Wilde, Thomas, 42
Wilde, Willie, 50, 60, 73, 106–
  109, 114, 120, 124, 132,
  166–168, 173–175, 189, 190
Wilde, Sir William, 30, 42–46,
  48, 49, 56, 61, 65–87, 89–91,
  94, 97–106, 146, 147, 181,
  187, 190
Wills, W. G., 42, 179
Wilson, T. G., 45
Wiseman, Cardinal, 191
Without Apology, 125
Woman's World, 145, 150–160

Wood, Mrs. Henry, 113, 155
Woodcock, George, 34
Wordsworth, William, 52, 149
World, The, 106, 148, 193

Yates, Edmund, 149
Yeats, William Butler, 64, 121,
  154, 169, 180
Yelverton Case, 83
Yonge, Charlotte M., 113
Young Men's Christian Asso-
  ciation, 67, 91

Zozimus, 67